MONEY IN THE COMPUTER AGE

Frontispiece: To most people, this is money. These crisp and finely printed bank-notes and discs of silvery, brassy, or coppery metal bearing the Queen's head are the reward for hours of toil and sweat in factory and office, shop and ship, and are the workaday aim of countless salary and wage earners. This money is cash and it may gradually disappear altogether with the increasing popularity of computer-centred credit transfer automation such as the National Giro Centre, the Joint Stock Banks' free credit transfer service, and the American Bankers' Association's ideas of a cashless world dependent upon telephone-line money cards. The United Kingdom is in the throes of the greatest monetary upheaval in its history, when both coinage and banking systems shaped by historical events are being replaced by scientifically derived systems entirely compatible with the demands of the twentieth century and beyond.

MONEY IN THE COMPUTER AGE

BY

Francis Paul

F. P. THOMSON, C.ENG., M.I.E.R.E., M.I.T.E.

—whose first book helped to persuade
Parliament to legislate for the National Giro

1966
THE QUEEN'S AWARD
TO INDUSTRY 1966

PERGAMON PRESS

OXFORD · LONDON · EDINBURGH · NEW YORK
TORONTO · SYDNEY · PARIS · BRAUNSCHWEIG

PERGAMON PRESS LTD.,
Headington Hill Hall, Oxford
4 & 5 Fitzroy Square, London W.1
PERGAMON PRESS (SCOTLAND) LTD.,
2 & 3 Teviot Place, Edinburgh 1
PERGAMON PRESS INC.,
44–01 21st Street, Long Island City, New York 11101
PERGAMON OF CANADA LTD.,
207 Queen's Quay West, Toronto 1
PERGAMON PRESS (AUST.) PTY. LTD.,
19a Boundary Street, Rushcutters Bay, N.S.W. 2011
PERGAMON PRESS S.A.R.L.,
24 rue des Écoles, Paris 5e
VIEWEG & SOHN GMBH,
Burgplatz 1, Braunschweig

Printed in Great Britain by A. Wheaton & Co., Exeter

Contents

Preface

A WEEK after the American spacecraft *Mariner IV* cruised to within 6118 miles of Mars and gave man his first close-up glimpse of the planet which earlier had inspired the novelist, H. G. Wells, to write his vision of a war of the worlds, the British Postmaster-General, on 21 July 1965, set his seal of approval on a far-reaching reform. This reform will influence the life of every man, woman, and child in Britain for many years after the exploits of *Mariner IV* and its successors have passed into limbo.

Fourteen years before H. G. Wells's story of a Martian invasion of Earth had captivated the adventurous mind of the youth of the 1890's, a Dr. Georg Coch of Austria devised a banking system of outstanding success in helping his country to survive a financial crisis. By 1942 every progressive west European continental country had recognised the exceptional merits of the post office giro originated in Vienna in 1883, and had adopted the principles in a version suited to the particular requirements of its own national economy.

By 1965 Britain's increasing integration with continental Europe through the European Free Trade Association, North Atlantic Treaty Organisation obligations, and through exploratory discussions regarding the possibility of joining the European Economic Community, was emphasising the incongruity of British monetary transmission systems. Whilst other advanced European civilisations were daily reaping the benefits of both a decimal currency and a computer-centred method of monetary transmission by giro, Britain was struggling along with archaic and cumbersome methods decided more by historical events than by scientific planning.

My first book, *Giro Credit Transfer Systems*, was written to heat up the campaign for the establishment of a British Giro and, consequently, was directed principally for the attention of government officials, bankers and businessmen, chambers of commerce, professional economists, and those members of the public who were growing increasingly uneasy about Britain's backwardness and the effect it was having on national efficiency and industrial production costs.

This book has been written to provide a record of the evolution of money and the influences brought to bear on its shape and handling methods by technologically inspired pressures. It is also a record of the Giro Campaign achievement, and outlines some of the arguments which should help progressive people—whether or not they are economists or technologists—to win a similar reform for countries as yet without this essential national service. It promises a solution to some of the problems confronting American business organisation.

A complete treatment is impossible in a book of this size, so the aim has been to provide an introduction to a subject so far little touched by authors, and to do it in language which encourages the general reader or student to explore the fascinating story of money and the changes it is undergoing to meet the challenges of the modern world.

In a period lasting barely 3 years, Britain's traditional banking and currency systems are undergoing changes the like of which have never before been experienced. First the National Giro, and then the introduction of decimal currency, will produce changes that no other nation has accommodated in such a short time. But without these reforms we would be unwise to view with equanimity the last third of this century and beyond. The decision to accommodate these far-reaching reforms in barely 3 years is a measure of British determination to do more than modernise outmoded methods; it is a sign of determination to utilise to the fullest extent the economically beneficial potentials of electronically controlled computer systems for the advancement of public welfare.

I am much indebted to N. Skene Smith, Esq., B.Com., the former Vice-Principal of the City of Birmingham College of

Commerce, for the stimulating suggestions he made during the preparation of both this book and of *Giro Credit Transfer Systems*.

I wish to record with a deep sense of appreciation the massive help given in making translations, undertaking research, and checking the manuscript, by my wife, Mrs. E. Sylvia Thomson, D.E.S., Dipl. Soc. (Stockholm), Dipl. Soc. (London), F.R.G.S.

Watford   F.P.T.
Herts.

Acknowledgements

THE writing of this book would have been impossible without help freely given by a large number of government and other organisations in many parts of the world and without the help and encouragement given by many individuals.

I would like to acknowledge with grateful thanks the continuing aid given for so many years by the Post Office authorities of: Austria, Belgium, Finland, France, West Germany, Holland, Israel, Italy, Japan, Luxembourg, Morocco, Norway, Sweden, Switzerland, and by officials of the Universal Postal Union.

Banking institutions of the United States of America, such as the American Bankers' Association, the Federal Reserve Banks of Minneapolis, New York, and Richmond, and the National Association of Mutual Savings Banks supplied literature and replied most helpfully to my inquiries about monetary problems. The American Management Association and the United States Post Office also sent valuable documentation. The headquarters of the Federal Reserve System, in Washington, D.C., was another source of unstinting help.

Appreciation has been expressed in the main body of the book to the British Members of Parliament who gave me valuable counsel and encouragement to continue the struggle for a British Giro and then, when victory was achieved in Parliament, either gave their permission for some of the letters they wrote to me to be reproduced or wrote special short articles for this book so it would, indeed, be a record of this important reform.

I have to acknowledge with thanks permission to reproduce illustrations provided from the following sources: the Central Office of Information: *Frontispiece*, Figs. 4, 5, 13. Thomas de la Rue & Co.: Figs. 1, 2, 12. Pergamon Press: Fig. 3. The Trustees of the British Museum: Fig. 6. The Comptroller of Her Majesty's Stationery Office: Fig. 7. Bankmuseet, Svenska Handelsbanken: Fig. 8. Historiska Museet, Stockholm: Figs. 9, 10. Antikvarisk-Topografiska Arkivet, Sweden: Fig. 11. The Committee of the London Clearing Banks: Fig. 16. The Federal Reserve Bank of Minneapolis, U.S.A.: Fig. 17. The Postmaster-General: Fig. 20. The *Sunday Express*: Fig. 21. The Ministry of Public Building and Works: Fig. 23. The Swedish Postbanken: Figs. 26, 27, 32–4, 45, 47. *Watford Post*: Fig. 41. English Electric Computer Co.: Fig. 44. Recognition Equipment Co.: Fig. 46. *The Sub-Postmaster*: Fig. 48. Figs. 36–40 and 42–3 are copyright controlled by the gentlemen depicted. Mullard Ltd.: Fig. 49.

I want to record my heartfelt thanks to the many organisations such as rotary clubs, consumer groups, etc., which invited me to lecture to them on giro during the campaign and whose continuing interest resulted in the suggestion that this book, a sequel to *Giro Credit Transfer Systems*, should be written as an omnibus record of the Giro Campaign organisation and achievement, with hints on how progressives in other countries— particularly North America—might benefit from establishing a similar system. Acknowledgement must also be made to those who demanded a book to stimulate discussion about giro's effect on the daily living conditions of the public; also to those teachers of physics and economics, current affairs, general and liberal studies, who asked me to provide a text book that would put the overall effects of discarding the monetary and banking systems of the past against a background of the computer-centred giro and decimal systems of the 1970's and beyond. And so, to friends and acquaintances in professional institutions and business associations, universities and colleges of technology and training, neighbourhood societies, etc., I say "Thank you".

Watford   F.P.T.
Herts.

CHAPTER 1

Money in a World of Technological Advance

MONETARY evolution has been progressing for about 10 000 years and has reached a stage when changes will be as dramatic as when shell and skin money disappeared in favour of metallic discs.

Money is the most universally recognised token of wealth and value and the common factor of nearly all professional and business transactions, as it is also of the majority of private ones. It is such a familiar characteristic of our daily life that we tend to ignore its fullest significance. Too often we think of money as being merely the bank-notes and coins which slip through our fingers, in and out of our pocket or purse; we are only worried if we do not get enough, or if what we have is lost or stolen.

Bank-notes and coins are such a familiar part of the domestic scene that we are likely to think of them or cash—as they are collectively called—as being the main kind of money. We are apt to regard private or public bank deposits as being too ethereal, although we often talk of going to the bank to get some money, meaning that cash will be supplied in return for a cheque drawn on our current account. The popularity of cash has rather over-shadowed other types of money, such as bank deposits, and this popularity has been engendered by the ease with which small pay-ments can be made as well as by the sense of tangible possession produced by the sight and feel of gaily patterned, crisp bank-notes and the jingling of gleaming coins. Furthermore, a high propor-tion of wage and salary earners have refused payment except in cash because, in their view, payment by cheque and other types of credit transfer would involve them in using a banking system seemingly too exclusive, cumbrous, costly, and complicated. Though often tinged with old-fashioned working-class prejudice against banking institutions—which to many poorer people have in the past been symbolic of ruthless capitalistic exploitation of the masses—these views are partly true; until recently many people have been the victims of an archaic banking system which only now has been making strenuous attempts to modernise itself. With this modernisation, aided by parliamentary legislation for the National Giro, comes the need to make monetary methods compatible with the scientifically evolved national economic and business management systems which, worked in sympathetic cohesion, will at last enable us to exploit the rewards of technological advance in the service of greater human happiness and prosperity.

1.1.   Monetary Evolution and a Computer-centred Civilisation

To appreciate what will be the shape of money in tomorrow's world and why it will be both socially desirable and altogether safer if cash gradually disappears in large measure, it is essential that we should recognise money for what it is. To do this we must know about its development and functions and why it has grown increasingly complex with the advance of civilisation, and we must understand that it is a medium that cannot be abolished at the behest of any political system.

Money is an international medium, so what is said of British money is also true of all countries' money and, in this, our assessment of what is scientifically advantageous will ultimately affect everybody.

One of the stranger characteristics of money as it is popularly expressed and used is that, although its acquisition is the primary aim of many people, their possession of it seems less like a personal possession than some other of their prized valuables. This feeling results from four main characteristics of money when held as cash, as a security, or as a bank deposit:

1. It cannot be moulded to reflect the personality of the possessor unless used to purchase goods or services.
2. Its exclusive identity with the possessor is impossible because it is legally taboo to mark bank-notes and coins with a personal emblem, and impossible to attach personality to a bank deposit except by giving it the name of the depositor.
3. Cash cannot be identified positively with a particular person because of 2 above and therefore is more difficult—compared with other valuable possessions—for the rightful owner of lost or stolen bank-notes and coins to identify. In general, identification is only possible as the result of circumstantial evidence such as fingerprints, the association of a wallet, purse, or other easily recognised personal possession, or the conditions under which the loss took place. No person can say "Those bank-notes and coins are mine; they have my mark on them" as he can say, for example, of stolen jewellery. It would be too laborious to require every possessor of bank-notes to keep a record of serial numbers.
4. Cash does not increase in value of itself as a result of careful tending by the owner. He may increase the value of neglected gold and silver plate by hammering out the dents and polishing it to a fine lustre, or by skilfully repairing and varnishing a battered canvas painted by a famous artist. No amount of straightening twisted coins and polishing them will increase their face value. Not even when a particular coin is withdrawn from circulation and is no longer legal tender does its scarcity value as a curio increase appreciably above its face value; the minting of a particular coinage is usually so vast and the rate of wear so slow that value increase for all practical purposes may be discounted.

Coins have served the needs of a developing world for a little less than 3000 years, and bank-notes were invented to meet a specific need in more recent times. The recent modernisation in banking methods suggests that both are nearing the end of popular usefulness.

Since about the start of the Industrial Revolution the circulation of money in its more popular forms has gradually extended to all sections of the community in ever-increasing volume instead of being restricted to a comparatively few wealthy groups, as it was until the Middle Ages. This vast extent in circulation, coupled with the needs of the machinery of national government and economic and social growth, very forcibly imposes questions as to the validity of the methods by which money is circulated and the shape it should take in a society which is increasingly dependent for its survival upon scientifically estimated planning.

In considering the practicability of cash in the modern world we must ask ourselves whether the scraps of synthetic parchment we call bank-notes—the duplication of which does not deter counterfeiters—are the best tokens of one very popular type of money. And are the discs of metal we call coins the best way to utilise several thousand tons of industrially valuable metals? Is the repeated counting and checking of bank-notes and coins and their costly storage in money-boxes, safes, and vaults the best way to employ the skill of thousands of intelligent people? Are these materials, methods, and manpower-consumption characteristics of modern monetary practice an essential concomitant of efficient business enterprise, or is it all an appalling waste of resources?

The answer can be found only in the extent to which the progress of civilisation is impeded. In recent years it has been shown that without a change in monetary methods there is a slowing down in development because the exploitation of technology is impeded, and that, unless we are prepared to substitute more efficient means than the large-scale handling of cash—to which we have been so accustomed in the past—economic progress, will suffer.

If we are to build a new world it will be necessary to substitute a vast increase in credit transfers for cash-handling, to encourage everybody to accept the "ethereal" money of bank deposits in place of bank-note handling, and to realise that invested money—as time deposits—is both a socially more desirable and a safer way to hold money than by jingling coins in pocket and purse. With this change will come a vast saving in raw materials, a great reduction in crimes—many of violence against the person—involving money, and the virtual elimination of dead-end and boring jobs in banking, accountancy, sales organisation, and many other office functions.

Between 1968 and 1972 we are in process of making this new world a reality. The establishment of the British National Giro and its reaction on private banking reform is setting the pace and evolving a plan that, by the end of the century, is likely to result in the development of a largely cashless society; one in which a satelite-communication-interlinked national and international giro-like network will activate banking methods, and peoples' daily purchase requirements are taken care of by the use of credit and money cards. The majority of other western European countries have operated giro systems for years past and, regarding our banking system in much the same light as we tend to regard the "backward" ways of developing countries in Africa and Asia, they have wondered how our economy has survived whilst we have tolerated so many archaic and cumbersome methods of monetary movement. After the establishment of the British National Giro, the second great reform will be the introduction of decimal currency; this is a reform—like giro—that will bring us into line with what our continental neighbours have enjoyed and benefited from throughout many of the years that we in Britain have been striving to make an outworn set of historical, rather than scientifically planned systems, perform all the requirements of a great industrial nation.

That we have a built-in resistance against change there can be little doubt. As long ago as 1894 the classic *Dictionary of Political Economy* observed (published by Macmillan, vol. 1, p. 514):

"Viewed from an economical standpoint, the non-adoption in a compulsory manner of any decimal or metric system of current money, weights, and measures, throughout the British Empire is one of the most glaring examples of national waste, financially and educationally, that the spirit of unwillingness to face the trouble of a change from old ways has ever inflicted."

The change to decimalisation has been equated by one reliable authority as a saving of 18 months' work in the life of every school child. In the government publication *Decimal Currency in the United Kingdom* is the statement (published by HMSO in 1966, pp. 3–4):

"... Much time in primary schools is devoted to teaching children the special rules of money arithmetic. When a child has learned the basic decimal processes of addition, subtraction, multiplication and division, he has to learn different methods for dealing with money sums; the process is tedious, time-consuming and lacking in intellectual excitement. When we have a decimal currency, teaching time will be saved and text books will be simplified. Some of the early disenchantment with mathematics often experienced by school children may be avoided, and the change will fit in well with changes already taking place in mathematics teaching.

"The benefits . . . will undoubtedly lead to substantial savings of time and effort in offices, banks, shops, and schools. Although these savings are important, there is no easy way of expressing them in money terms. So far as office work is concerned, the Institute of Office Management told the Halsbury Committee that they believed it likely that the cost of change-over in offices would be recouped in savings within a year or so from the date of change. For schools, the saving in mathematics teaching time for the 6 to 11 age group has been estimated at roughly 5 per cent to 10 per cent, or 2 per cent of total teaching time."

Whilst the introduction of decimal currency will bring Britain into line with the customs of other countries, the world itself is gradually moving towards a cashless system. By the end of the twentieth century, bank-notes and coins may be as rare as motor-cars were on the streets of our towns in 1914, and our ability to change may even yet defy the sceptics who have prophesied that even in 1999 wage-earners will still insist that their wages be paid so that they can see and feel their money trickling through their fingers.

We must not forget our grandfathers' courageous defiance of the sceptics who decreed the ruin of British economy if the cart-horse was ever swept from the streets in favour of horseless carriages, for:

". . . no man can survive without the horse and the country's ruination would be complete without this animal, which so willingly carries us where we please, and is so modest in his demands on us for food and shelter. At the end of his long span of uncomplaining useful life his flesh feeds the poor; his hair fills the best mattresses and makes the longest-wearing brushes and brooms; his hide is the most prized cover for highest quality furniture, and shoes the people; his hooves are indispensable for glue and for the making of handles of quality, and for orna-ment; his bones are ground and make the finest fertiliser; and his entrails supply physicians with potions and the cats of Kensington and Mayfair with tasty meals."

Let us now decide what is really meant by *money*.

1.2. The Development and Functions of Money

The danger of thinking of money as being merely bank-notes and coins is that, to its owner, its most important feature is not its quantity but its purchasing power; that is the quantity of goods and services for which it will exchange and in this function it may take more—or less—cash to achieve the same result as formerly. Even the purchasing power of pure gold varies over a period and for that reason in our internal trade it is no longer used. But in our national reserves gold is still very important as a means of meeting payments abroad and to support the external value of the pound sterling.

Anything can be money, and one of the difficulties of establish-ing a definition of it is that almost everything has been money during the last 10 000 years. There are obvious advantages in choosing materials which alter little with wear and handling, and which do not deteriorate with exposure, ageing, and chemical action.

Mankind's first need was for a system of easy exchange within the community, and probably dates from about the time our ancestors started to make tools. It is the belief of some authorities that early man had few if any personal possessions and all goods—sometimes even wives—were owned by the tribe. A study of primitive peoples surviving into the twentieth century suggests that communities only gradually evolved a money-like system.

The earliest flint tools discovered in Britain are large and crude and date from about 350 000 B.C., when these islands were joined by a land bridge to continental Europe, and ice-age glaciers still covered all but the southern coastal areas.

From this time onwards the need for a primitive type of money may have developed. By 7500 B.C. lake-dwellers at Star Carr in Yorkshire had arrived at an evolutionary stage of using fine tools to carve bone and antlers.

It is well recognised that when life in a primitive community was extremely hard and the struggle to live so great that neither time nor energy were available for pursuits other than the fight for food, shelter, and physical being, that all—or practically all—community effort had to be concentrated on these essentials. Therefore man's struggle for existence in the Britain of 10 000 or more years ago would be one of constant battle against the effects of an inhospitable climate, wild animals, marauders from other tribes, and unpredictable natural conditions. There would be recurrent disease to lay waste his efforts and, often enough, the herbal and other potions that at one time seemed to heal and bring him fortune would the next time react against him. If time was to be made for bone and antler carving and other pursuits not strictly concerned with the struggle for existence, it would have been necessary to arrange a sharing of community responsibility so that men could take work best suited to their natural prowess. Specialisation with mutual interdependence on others would result, and the hunter of animals for meat and skins would have to negotiate for arrows and spears with the skilled flint-chippers. A simple monetary system would have its origins in the hunter's need to debit his waste of arrows and spear-heads when he returned empty-handed against the days when he returned with an abundance of carcasses. To prevent the outbreak of recrimination when a skin was badly damaged as a result of the way the animal was killed, the hunter might agree to provide some other article or service to make a fair balance in the estimation of the tribal community, thus laying the foundations of a system in which a skin was accepted as having a value in terms of other money-like objects. Those appointed to undertake the creative tasks of the community would very likely be regarded by the warriors and the hunters as having a softer life and, unless there was some primitive monetary system to safeguard their interests, they might easily be discounted in times of stress.

A scribe of ancient Egypt's twelfth dynasty described the way in which a cloth-weaver in that civilisation's moneyless economy earned his keep; the following quotation is taken from *A History of Tapestry*, by W. G. Thomson (published by Hodder & Stoughton, second edition, p. 3):

> "The weaver in the interior of the house is more unfortunate than a woman. His knees are at the height of his head. He breathes no fresh air. If for a single day he cannot make the regulation quantity of cloth he is tied to the loom like the lotus of the marsh. It is only by giving presents of bread to the keeper of the door that he is allowed to see the light of day."

Egyptian workers of 2000 B.C. were paid in goods and food rations, and a bribe of bread was the only way to escape completion of a task assignment.

Skins were widely accepted as money in early times. The Estonian *râha* means money, but in a Lapp dialect of northern Scandinavia it also means skin. In the same part of Scandinavia a packet of forty skins was called a *zimmer* and within living memory has taken the place of coins. In western Russia, until the fourteenth century, the fur of black marmot was used as money and called a *kuna*. In Mongolia, Alaska, and Canada, skins have taken the place of money within the last century. And, paradoxically, in the island of New Caledonia—about 1000 miles east of the Queensland coast of Australia—flying fox fur money has, in less than 50 years, given way to an efficient and thriving post office giro.

A clear distinction between barter and money did not come until the acceptance within a community that a particular article possessed a certain value in relation to other articles, although this monetary value might be upset by an accidental shortage or glut of the monetary unit article(s). In some primitive communities some money-like articles were reserved for ceremonial occasions or for special purposes, such as the sperm-whale tooth used until the nineteenth century by the Fijians to purchase a bride or a large canoe, or to discharge a debt resulting from the murder of a man.

Preceding the invention of coins and—in many parts of the world—continuing long after their acceptance by developing civilisations, cowrie shells were used as money in Thailand; fish-hooks were legal tender in the Gilbert Islands; long-tusked boars were the money of the New Hebrides; tea-bricks were thus used in China; grain in India; salt in Ethiopia; cocoa beans in Mexico; sheep and goats in Kenya; snail shells in Paraguay; iron bars in France; butter in Norway; bars shaped like partly completed swords in Britain; edible rats in Easter Island; and traders' beads in Africa and Canada. These are but a few of the strange objects used for money in many parts of the world from ancient times until, in some developing countries, the nineteenth century and later (Fig. 1).

FIG. 1. Money can be anything and has been almost everything during the 10 000 or so years of its development. Primitive peoples chose ornaments or articles of use, of which a few examples are illustrated. At the top left corner is ceremonial currency from the Fiji Islands: a whale's tooth. Below, a purse of shell money and a dog's tooth from the Solomon Islands. In the centre, a string of *diwarra* or nassa shells from New Britain; the shells are like cowries and about 0.37 inch long. The collection is completed by shell ring money from New Guinea, and cowrie shell money from Africa and Polynesia.

Fig. 1

1.3. The Definition of Money

The definition usually given by dictionaries is that money is any material serving by agreement as a common medium of exchange and as a measure of value in trade.

The term appeared first as *mynet*, in the Anglo–Saxon laws of King Athelstan of England (reigned A.D. 924–39). In writings dating from A.D. 1300 it appears as *mone*.

But a comprehensive definition of money is possible only in terms of the functions it performs. It has been shown that the first need of money probably was as an exchange medium to relate the value of commodities in a primitive community. As civilisation grew more complex, money was called upon to perform other functions as well.

1.3.1. THE FUNCTIONS OF MONEY

The economist looks on the functions of money as being primarily those of:

1. A medium of exchange.
2. A unit of account.
3. A store of value.

Broadly, money represents debts from or claims on individuals and institutions in society, or purchasing power. It is held simply for hoarding; or as a precaution against having to spend in the near future; or as a means of meeting definite future private or business expenditure; or to enable holders of money to buy goods, services, or securities which they think (or speculate) will rise in price, i.e. value in terms of money, in the future. Whether in the form of cash (i.e. coins and bank-notes) or bank deposits, money is the only universally accepted medium of exchange and, there-fore, the only completely liquid asset. It is neither a production good nor a consumption good. Its value, or purchasing power, depends upon the quantity that is offered in exchange for the quantity of goods, services, and securities offered on the market.

When more money is offered (as when goods are in short supply) the value of money tends to fall; that is to say, the prices of the goods, services, and securities tend to rise, i.e. a rise in prices is equivalent to a fall in the value of money. The value of money tends to fall when wages or salaries are increased in response to demand because the same amount of work is being done but at a higher level of cost, with the result that the product is more expensive.

The purchasing power of money can be transferred to others—either permanently or on loan—to induce them (or help them) to produce goods or services, to pay for goods, services, and securities already available, as a reward, as compensation, or simply as a straight gift.

Briefly, the functions of money may be summarised as:

(a) A measure of value.
(b) A medium of exchange.
(c) A means of discharging a debt.
(d) A method of distinguishing the worth of articles and services by giving them a price.
(e) A means of hoarding wealth.
(f) A way of accumulating value.
(g) A reserve of purchasing power.
(h) A status symbol.
(i) A unit of account in which costs are expressed and services are rendered.
(j) A means of inducement.
(k) A measure of productivity.
(l) A form of compensation for loss or injury.

The wheel has been called mankind's earliest invention still in everyday use. Possibly it was the first invention to provide mechanical advantage; some would claim that the lever and fulcrum preceded it, nevertheless. But whether the wheel or the lever and fulcrum was the first invention to help man build a civilisation, there is no doubt that money was in use long before the first log was used as a roller to facilitate the movement of heavy loads, or the first disc was sliced from a log to provide a chariot with wheels.

1.4. The Invention of Coins

Until primitive man had discovered metals and how to refine and work them, and how to engrave or emboss many similar pieces of metal of the same intrinsic value with identical signs or symbols denoting authority and value as money, coinage as we know it today did not exist. As every metal-worker knows, it is relatively easy to make a single model of a new design; the problems of fabrication multiply enormously when several hundred or more identical articles have to be made.

If we consider the scanty knowledge of metals then available and the primitive means of recording and of communicating information, the taboos and the prohibitions which are likely to have inhibited workers' activities, the absence of facilities for experiment with scientifically reliable assessment of results, and the poor tools and fabrication equipment available at the time, it is in every respect amazing that between about 2250 and 2150 B.C. the Assyrians of Cappadocia developed a means of making silver ingots which they embossed—to confirm authorisation— with the seal of their state authority. In his massively comprehensive book on *Primitive Money* (published by Pergamon, second edition, p. 209), Paul Einzig states:

"Early documents from Cappadocia frequently refer to payments of sums that have been paid or are to be paid in money 'of my seal', 'of your seal', 'of the seal of so-and-so'. Sidney Smith suggests that some ingots were stamped by a State authority, and that they changed hands above their actual metallic value. He bases this claim on the text of a bill of exchange which stipulates that if payment of the sum of 42 *minae* of refined silver is not made in 230 days after a certain date, interest shall be paid at the rate of 1 *shekel* per *mina* per month. "On a *mina* of the house of Garu (a kind of magistrate)

they shall return one and one-eighth *shekels* and pay the silver."
This seems to indicate that for officially stamped silver there is
an additional interest or premium of 1/8 *shekel* per *mina*. If this
interpretation is correct it means that monetary metal of
guaranteed fineness was lent at a higher rate of interest. What
matters is that at that early period there were silver ingots in
use with official seals.

"On the ground of this evidence, credit for the invention of
State-guaranteed money must be given to Cappadocia. Her
stamped silver ignots differ from the gold dumps produced by
the King of Lydia 1500 years later in degree only. There is no
evidence whether the officially stamped Cappadocian ingots
aimed at uniformity in weight, and whether the seal of the
magistrate guaranteed a certain standard fineness. In any case,
since the early coins changed hands mostly by weight they did
not differ fundamentally from officially sealed ingots; and the
fineness of early coins also varied widely.

"Although there is no evidence to show whether the officially
stamped silver ingots were legal tender in Cappadocia, there
was obviously no need for making their acceptance compulsory,
since they actually commanded a premium against privately
stamped ingots.

"The metals used for monetary purposes were pre-eminently
silver and copper."

Despite the advanced civilisation attained by the Ancient
Egyptians, the development of a guaranteed monetary system
seems to have been unnecessary due to the existence of an early
form of government-planned economy, although Mr. Einzig draws
attention in his book (p. 194) to the suggestion that:

". . . a monetary system is claimed to have been in operation
during the earliest period of recorded history. King Menes, of
the Ist Dynasty, at the end of the fourth millennium B.C., is
said to have fixed legal value for small 14 gram gold bars
marked with his name. It has also been suggested that under
the kings of the IVth and VIth Dynasties gold rings were

produced with a uniform weight closely approximating to that of the bar of Menes. [C. H. V. Sutherland, *Gold* (London, 1959), p. 31.] Even if these bars and rings served a monetary purpose there is no evidence for their monetary use during more recent times."

Wall paintings in tombs suggest that ancient Egyptians exchanged gold and bronze rings for goods and to settle debts, and that barter was used concurrently as a means of trade promotion. A painting in a tomb dating from about 2400 B.C. depicts a bartering scene in a sequence of four stages. In the tomb of Mebamun at Thebes, dated about 1380 B.C., goldsmiths are shown weighing gold rings against the weight of a ram's head. A great wall painting, now in the British Museum in London, depicts Nubians paying tribute in gold rings to their Egyptian masters.

Gold and silver were used from the earliest times as measures of value in the Eastern Mediterranean area, and there is evidence that the Chaldeans of Ur imported gold from India for this purpose. In the Bible, in the Old Testament Book of Genesis (ch. 13, v. 2), appears the following statement:

"And Abram was very rich in cattle, in silver, and in gold."

After his wife Sarah died at the age of 127 years in Canaan, Abram negotiated with Ephron for a burial place for her (ch. 23, vs. 13–15):

"And he spake unto Ephron in the audience of the people of the land, saying, But if thou wilt give it, I pray thee, hear me: I will give thee money for the field; take it of me, and I will bury my dead there.

"And Ephron answered Abram, saying unto him,

"My lord, hearken unto me: the land is worth four hundred shekels of silver; what is that betwixt me and thee? bury therefore thy dead.

"And Abram hearkened unto Ephron; and Abram weighed to Ephron the silver, which he had named in the audience of

the sons of Heth, four hundred shekels of silver, current money
with the merchant.''

If the money of the time had been in coins the value would have
been obvious from the embossed or engraved mark of authority
on each, and Abram would have been spared the trouble of using
his scales to weigh the silver.

Despite the pioneering activities of Cappadocia in the establishment of a state-guaranteed currency, many experts attribute the
adjacent westerly kingdom of Lydia with the invention of coins.
Both are part of modern Turkish Anatolia.

About 700 B.C. the Lydians mined a natural amalgam they
called *electrum*. It comprised approximately 73 per cent gold and
27 per cent silver. In the reign of Lydia's legendary King Gyges
(686–656 B.C.), ingots of electrum—sometimes called *white gold*—
were impressed with rudely shaped unengraved punches placed
on either side to receive blows from a hammer. These punch-
marks signified official authorisation as currency. But soon the
embosser started to adorn ingots with the badge of the authority
under whose auspices the currency was issued. From Lydia
coinage spread as a valuable ingredient of business organisation.
The Greeks substituted engraved dies for the primitive punches
and included the name of the ruler or authority issuing the coins.

The earliest coins were bean-shaped or oval and were embossed
with a mark depicting an animal or its foreparts, the sunk centre
of the coin and its irregular edges giving it a seal-like appearance.
Later coins were engraved with a figure of a god or of a man.
Compared with the mark of authority on the Cappadocian currency, the Lydian was a great advance because its mark of authority was a guarantee of both weight and value (Figs. 2 and 3).

Coinage originated independently in China about the same time
as in Lydia, and spread into Japan and Korea.

The Bible's first reference to coins appears in the Old Testament
mention of their use by the Persians. It is known that Lydian
techniques spread to both Persia and India and, about 400 B.C.,
the Romans laid the foundations of modern coin minting.

1.5. Britain's Coinage

Gold, silver, and other base metals were worked by the inhabitants of Britain long before the Roman invasion. There is
evidence of a fairly free exchange of knowledge between the
Belgic metal-smiths of continental Europe's western seaboard and
Britain's south-east coast inhabitants, who began to strike gold
coins about 150 B.C. These coins bore an impression on one side
of a laureate head and on the reverse a horse or a chariot. In his
book *The Ancient Stones of Scotland*, Professor W. Douglas
Simpson states (p. 78): ". . . the legends on ancient British coins
and other evidence prove that Latin was understood in the south
of England before the Roman conquest."

So there is the intriguing idea that early British coinage may
have been influenced as much by Lydian and Greek developments
as by the skills the Romans brought with them much later. During
excavations of Bronze and Iron Age remains in a cave at Covesea,
near Lossiemouth, on the Morayshire coast of Scotland, it was
found that later inhabitants had used Roman pottery and
brooches, and had made barbarous imitations of Roman coins;
the cave also contained pre-Christian sculptures. British coinage
ended with the invasion of the Roman Emperor Claudius, and

FIG. 2. Here are illustrations of some of the earliest coins. At the top left is
the *first brass* (A.D. 138–61), issued by Antonius Pius to commemorate the
Roman Conquest of Britain; on this, the reverse side, is the first impression
of Britannia and the prototype of the image on present-day pennies. To the
right is a Roman *denarius*, the *D*. or *d*. still being used as an abbreviation
for *penny*. At the top right is a *decadrachm* of Carthage (241–146 B.C.); the
reverse side is shown. The two small coins at the left centre are also *denarius*,
but showing the reverse (top) and face sides. At the centre is the Owl of
Athens on the *tetradrachm* (490–407 B.C.). At the right centre is the Shield of
Thebes (426–395 B.C.). At the bottom left corner is a large coin, the *decadrachm*
of Syracuse (407–357 B.C.). To the right centre of the *decadrachm* is a *stater*
(350–300 B.C.) with the Pegasus of Corinth. The bottom centre coin is the
Turtle of Aegina (650–600 B.C.). At the right lower corner is the *Ear of Barley*
of Metapontum (330–300 B.C.). To appreciate fully the amazing skill of the
Greek and Roman minters of these coins, whose tools and knowledge of
metals must have been primitive by modern standards, a modern student of
technology should try making replicas.

Fig. 2

the first coin of significance after that time was the so-called *ear of barley*, minted in Colchester from about 5 B.C. to A.D. 43.

Roman conquerors of Britain progressively suppressed native

FIG. 3. The colophon of Pergamon Press is taken from this Greek coin dating from about 400 B.C., and found at Heraklea. The head is of Athena, the goddess of the intellectual arts.

mints and replaced them with those established, for example, by Emperor Marcus Aurelius Carausius, one of which was in London.

By the reign of King Alfred the Great (A.D. 871–99) at least eight mints were operating and, by the time of the Norman Conquest (A.D. 1066), many English towns had appointed their

own "moneyers" to produce coinage for local use. This cu
gave the towns prestige and also helped to defeat the activiti
highwaymen and thieves. When national communications were
so bad, the chances of apprehending criminals were very poor
unless the area of their operations could be restricted. By coining
money locally there was more chance of catching men who had
robbed travellers and citizens of money, for it would be immediately evident if a stranger was seen to be spending money
for which he could not account and which bore the mark of
another district.

From the sixteenth century until 1812 the minting of gold and
silver was almost exclusively confined to the Royal Mint in the
Tower of London. In the latter year the Mint was moved to the
building shown in Fig. 4, on Tower Hill, London. Now the Royal
Mint has been moved again. The first task of the new premises at
Swansea, south Wales, is the minting of Britain's decimal coinage.
What has been called "Birmingham's Mint" is a commercial
entity engaged largely in the production of coinage for the governments of oversea countries.

From the year A.D. 1526 until the nineteenth century, British
coins were usually made of gold, silver, and copper; the intrinsic
value and the face value were the same, with a gold standard of
916.6 parts per 1000, and a silver standard of 925 parts per 1000.
But from the start of the twentieth century, alloys such as bronze,
brass, and cupro–nickel were used instead. Gold coins were withdrawn from circulation in 1914 and, since 1946, no silver coins
have been distributed by the Royal Mint.

Numismatics is an immense subject and a complete treatment
is beyond the scope of this book. But there is advantage in knowing a little about the origins of coins in everyday use as well as
those famous in history. We would do well to bear in mind that
we are at the threshold of a British monetary system which has
evolved gradually over 2000 years and is being replaced by a
scientifically calculated system of coinage and banking. In less
than a century people will ask what was a florin as they now ask
what was a groat.

Rapidly increasing public interest in coins is evidenced by the growing number of coin shops springing up in British cities. In the early sixties there were not more than six in the whole of Britain, and coin collection was regarded as the Cinderella of popular hobbies. The growing interest seems almost to be ousting stamp-collecting, and during lecture tours the author has been asked numerous questions on the origins of coins and their names; also about monetary expressions which have caused confusion. The following collection comprises names and expressions that have puzzled either lecture audiences or the author.

1.6.   Coinage Names and Monetary Terms and Abbreviations

1. **Augustalle.** Following the revival of trade in western Europe from the eleventh century onwards, gold coins called *augustalles* were issued in A.D. 1231 by Emperor Frederik II of Germany. His example was followed by Genoa in 1252, by Venice in 1284, and by Florence in 1253 where the coin was called a *florin*.
2. **Awpenny, awpney.** Yorkshire (England) slang expressions meaning halfpenny.
3. **Bank-note.** A piece of paper money issued by a bank.
4. **Bank.** A place for the storage (depositing), paying out, and exchange of money. Ancillary services may include money-borrowing facilities and advisory services.
5. **Bank Clearing House.** A centre to which banks send cheques, etc., for clearance, which comprises the debiting and crediting of the amounts shown on the cheques against the

---

Fig. 4. The Royal Mint was built on London's Tower Hill during 1810–12 to the design of the architect of the British Museum—Sir Robert Smirke—and before that minting of coinage was carried out in the Tower of London itself. The Mint is under the control of the Chancellor of the Exchequer and is the centre for the production of all Britain's coinage and much of that used in Commonwealth and some foreign countries. By the 1970's the Royal Mint will have been re-established in larger premises in South Wales, where it will help to provide a greater variety of employment in a former mining area.

Fig. 4

banks whose customers have been concerned with the issue and receipt of the cheques.

6. **Bank, Federal Reserve.** A regional bank in the United States of America which performs the functions of 5 and of the Bank of England.

7. **Bezant, byzant.** A gold coin introduced by Constantine the Great; also called the *solidus*; it had a value of 72 to the £. Known as the *bezant* or *byzant* because of its Byzantine Empire origins, it also came into use in western Europe.

8. **Bob.** A slang name said to have originated during Sir Robert Walpole's lifetime (1676–1745) for the English shilling.

9. **Brass.** A colloquialism for money, usually referring to coins of lower value. In common use in the mid-fourteenth century, the term appears in Piers Plowman, "Beere heer bras on thi Bac."

10. **Buck.** Slang for an American dollar.

11. **Bull.** Slang of mid-seventeenth-century vintage for a half-crown.

12. **c.** The abbreviation for cent(s) (U.S.A.), and centime(s) (French-speaking countries). One *cent* is one-hundredth part of a larger value coin or monetary unit.

13. **Cash.** Originated in the sixteenth century from the French word *caisse*, meaning coffer or chest for the storage of money, the word means ready money or coin and banknotes immediately available. In *The Life of Henry King V*, by William Shakespeare (1564–1616), Act II, sc. 2, the soldier Nyn, of King Henry's army, asks another soldier, "I shall have my noble?" and Pistol replies, "In cash most justly paid."

14. **Cent.** See 12.

15. **Centime.** See 12. Also a coin of Holland.

16. **Check.** North American spelling of cheque.

17. **Cheque.** A written order to a bank ordering them to pay money.

18. **Coin.** A piece of material, usually metal but occasionally

wood or plastic, used as money. In the *Clerk's Tales* Geoffrey Chaucer (1340–1400) refers to a *coyn*.

19. **Coinage.** The processing of coins from the material of manufacture. The money thus made. A set of coins comprising the units of a particular monetary system.

20. **Coinage, Decimal.** A monetary system in which value is counted in units of 10 or one-tenth.

21. **Commodity.** An article of use usually in common demand, for example commercial or household goods.

22. **Copper.** A colloquialism for a British penny (1*d*.) coin.

23. **Counterfoil.** Part of a postal order, cheque, or order to pay money retained by the remitter as proof of his action in sanctioning the written instruction. Intended as a means of countering theft and fraud.

24. **Credit.** Reputation. Acknowledgement of possession. Proof of a good quality. A belief that a person or organisation can and will pay what he (they) promise to pay. A paper token of wealth either static or transferable.

25. **Credit card.** A card to confirm the creditworthiness of a person.

26. **Crown.** A coin first issued in England in 1551 and part of the third coinage of King Edward VI. It has not been distributed in quantity by the Royal Mint in recent times as it proved inconveniently large and heavy for twentieth-century use. Value: five shillings (5*s*.) (Fig. 5).

27. **Crown, Half.** A British coin with a value of two shillings and sixpence (2*s*. 6*d*.) (see Fig. 5).

28. **Crown, Double.** An English coin worth ten shillings (10*s*.) which was part of the second coinage of King James I (1603–25). Withdrawn from circulation many years ago.

29. **Currency.** An expression which came into use about 1740 to describe the circulation of money (i.e. bank-notes and coins).

30. **d.** Prefixed by a number this abbreviation indicates a penny or pennies. It is an abbreviation for *denarius*, a silver coin minted by the Romans nearly 2000 years ago (see Fig. 3).

31. **Daalder.** See 68.

32. **Debasement.** This is the reduction of the precious metal content of a coin to give it a lower value or to indicate its lowered purchasing value compared with a gold or other standard.

33. **Decimal currency.** See 20 and 29.

34. **Denarius.** See 30. The influence of Charlemagne (Charles the Great, 768–814) was sufficiently great for him to abandon the gold standard in favour of a monetary system based on the *denarius* or silver penny. A pound (or 1 *libra*) was equal to 20 *solidus* or to 240 *denarius*; i.e. 240 *denarius* in silver weighed one pound. Hence the origin of 240*d.* being equal to 20*s.* or £1. But both the £1 and shilling were moneys of account and did not exist as discrete coins. As the mints came under feudal control the pound-weight value of the *denarius* gradually depreciated.

35. **Denier.** The *denier* of Cologne, the *denier* of Paris (or *denier parisis*), and the denier of Tours (or *denier tournais*) were locally minted equivalents of the *denarius*.

Fig. 5. This was the coinage struck to commemorate the accession to the throne of Queen Elizabeth II in 1953. By 1975 this coinage will have been almost completely swept away by the introduction in 1971 of decimal currency. With the demise of the coinage shown here will go a link directly connecting the development of British coinage with roots extending back 1000 and more years. A description of each coin is given in this sequence: name; value; metallic composition; diameter in inches (in centimetres); weight in grains (in grams). The obverse (i.e. face) of the half-crown is similar to all other coins except the crown, and except for slight differences in the inscription surrounding the head of the Queen. *Top row:* Half-crown reverse and obverse; 2*s.* 6*d.*: cupro–nickel; 1.27 in. (3.23 cm); 218.18 gr. (14.14 g). Florin obverse; 2*s.*: cupro–nickel; 1.12 in. (2.85 cm); 174.54 gr. (11.31 g). *Middle row:* English shilling reverse; 1*s.*: cupro–nickel; 0.93 in. (2.36 cm); 87.23 gr. (5.66 g). Crown obverse and reverse; 5*s.*: cupro–nickel; 1.52 in. (3.86 cm); 436.36 gr. (28.28 g). Scottish shilling reverse: as English shilling. *Bottom row:* Sixpence reverse; 6*d.*: cupro–nickel; 0.76 in. (1.94 cm); 43.64 gr. (2.83 g). Threepence reverse; 3*d.*: brass, twelve-sided; 0.86 in. (2.2 cm) across corners; 0.83 in. (2.11 cm) across flats; 105 gr. (6.8 g). Penny reverse; 1*d.*: bronze; 1.21 in. (3.09 cm); 145.83 gr. (9.45 g). Halfpenny reverse; ½*d.*: bronze; 1.00 in. (2.55 cm); 87.5 gr. (5.67 g). Farthing reverse; ¼*d.*: bronze; 0.80 in. (2.02 cm); 43.75 gr. (2.84 g).

FIG. 5

36. **Deutschmark.** The monetary unit of post-war West Germany. Abbreviation: DM.

37. **Dollar.** The name of the monetary unit of several countries, notably the United States of America. The origin of *dollar* was *thaler*, a large and heavy silver coin of sixteenth-century Bohemia (see 68 and 10). Abbreviation: $.

38. **Double.** The Channel Islands have a coinage independent of Britain comprising 8, 4, 2 and 1 *double* pieces. The name was derived from the French *double denier* or *liard*, the successor to the older French *denier tournais* (see 35). A *double* is made of bronze and is the same size as an English penny.

39. **Double crown.** See 28.

40. **Doubloon.** An old Spanish coin made of gold.

41. **Ducat.** An Italian coin of the Middle Ages.

42. **Eight, Piece of.** A colloquialism for *peso*, the Spanish equivalent of a dollar; originally intended to be a weight in the shape of a silver bar. In the children's book *Treasure Island*, by Robert Louis Stevenson (1850–94), one of the characters—Long John Silver—has a parrot whose favourite call is, "Pieces of eight; pieces of eight". Many British children see the story as a pantomime or television play and learn this expression without finding out—even in adulthood—its meaning and origin (see 100).

43. **Escudos.** A Portuguese coin. Abbreviation: Esc. or $.

44. **Esterlings.** Emigrants from eastern Europe to England in the thirteenth century who were skilled in fine metalwork and were put to work to help regulate the coinage were known as *Esterlings*. Their abilities led to the adoption of the expression "esterling" as a term of perfection and this was gradually contracted to *sterling*. A writ issued at Chester, dated 16 August 1257, commanded the Mayor of London to proclaim to the City; "The gold money which the King has caused to be made should be immediately current there and elsewhere within the realm of England, in all transactions of buying and selling, at the rate of twenty pennies

of Sterlings for every gold penny." In many transactions
the weight of the silver pennies was accepted as a standard,
which resulted in the pound sterling becoming a recognised
standard.

45. **Farthing.** A bronze coin worth one-quarter of a British penny
and withdrawn from circulation in the mid-twentieth
century. Abbreviation: $\frac{1}{4}d$. (see Fig. 5). Farthings were first
minted in England during the reign of King Edward the
Confessor (1004–66). This coin is mentioned in the Anglo–
Saxon version of the Bible (St. Matthew, ch. 5, v. 26):
"Verily I say unto thee. Thou shalt by no means come out
thence, till thou hast paid the uttermost farthing." In old
times the coin was called *feorthing* or *fourthling*.

46. **Five sovereign.** See 110.

47. **Fiver** or **fivver.** Slang for a £5 bank-note.

48. **Florin.** In the year 1253 the Republic of Florence minted a
gold coin equivalent to the *augustalle* (see 1) and called it
first a *florentine* and then a *florin*. At first it corresponded
exactly to a *pound piccoli* or 240d. picc. (£1 picc.) the d.
being the abbreviation for *deniers* (see 30, 34–5), but as
silver depreciated in value the *florin* increased in value,
being of gold, and Florence developed two systems of
account: (a) based on the *florin*, of which a silver *florin*
worth one-tenth of the gold *florin* was minted, and (b)
based on the *petty denier*. In England in the year 1343,
during the reign of King Edward III (1312–77), a gold
florin was minted but did not remain in circulation for
long; the name was taken into English, however. The
silver *florin* of recent British coinage was first issued in
1849, 12 years after Queen Victoria (1837–1901) came to
the throne, with a view to establishing a decimal currency
system (see 20, 29). This silver coin had a value of two
shillings (2s.) and originally was known as the *godless* or
graceless coin because the inscription "Dei Gratia" was
omitted; about 750 000 coins were struck. The omission
was remedied in 1851 when a broader and thinner coin

was struck (see Fig. 5). Abbreviation: 2*s*. The Dutch *florin* is also known as a *guelder;* abbreviation: fl. or Gld.

49. **Franc.** A monetary unit of Belgium (abbreviation: Fr.); France, (F); Lichtenstein, (Fr); Luxembourg, (Fr); Switzerland, (Fr); etc. The *nouvelle franc* was the term given to the currency of France after General de Gaulle reorganised the currency shortly after he attained power in the 1950's. One NF was equal to 100 old francs.

50. **Giro.** The name of a simplified and scientifically planned banking system which has increasingly spread throughout the world since the beginning of the twentieth century. The word is derived from the Greek *guros* meaning ring, circle, or circuit.

51. **Giro centre.** A building sited at a geographically central place where optimum convenience and the maximum efficiency in communication with the area the giro is planned to cover will be achieved. The building usually has, in addition to excellent and inexpensive regional or national connexion potentials through the postal service, etc., a complex of electronically operated computers aided by automated document and other handling equipment which has the capability of rapidly processing the monetary transfer instructions and credit transfer documentation of both giro account holders and those who have ordered payments to them, and of rapidly issuing confirmatory notes or statements to parties concerned in each transaction.

52. **Giroist.** A giro account holder.

53. **Gold standard.** The standard of value which many nations have adopted when regulating the value of their monetary units. It has been said that the only true money is gold and all else is but a token of money. But in recent times it has been realised the value of money depends more upon the supply available and the demand of those willing to hold it. As long as supply is sufficiently limited and the people have sufficient confidence in the stability of its value *per*

unit (in terms of goods and services), this value will tend to be maintained.

54. **Gn.** or **gn.** or **gns.** Abbreviations for *guinea, guines,* or *guineas* (see 57).

55. **Groat.** An English small coin of silver struck between 1357–1662, and with a value of about 4*d*. Also identified with the British fourpenny silver coin struck between 1836–56. *Groat* has become synonymous with worthless.

56. **Guelder.** A monetary unit in Holland (see 48).

57. **Guinea.** First struck in 1663 and with a value of twenty shillings, but increased to twenty-one shillings in 1717, this coin was made of gold mined in Guinea and brought to England by the Company of Merchant Adventurers. It was suspended in 1813. The term *guinea* continued as an elegance in the fixing of prices for articles and services, and has continued to be used more particularly by the professional classes and by merchants seeking to attract the custom of the wealthy.

58. **Halfpenny.** The earliest English *halfpenny* comparable with those used in twentieth-century Britain was made of copper and undated; latterly it was made of bronze. Abbreviation: $\frac{1}{2}d$. Documents dating from the time of King Edward the Confessor mention halfpennies but these most likely were one-third pennies like those mentioned in the laws of King Alfred the Great (871–99).

59. **Half-sovereign.** See 111.

60. **Hape.** Scottish slang for a halfpenny.

61. **Happney.** Cornish slang for a halfpenny.

62. **Hawpenny.** Yorkshire slang for a halfpenny.

63. **Heads or harps.** The Irish equivalent of 64.

64. **Heads or tails.** An expression originating during the Roman conquest of Britain, when the toss of a coin determined whether an action should be implemented or not, except that the Romans used the expression *heads or ships*.

65. **Hog.** An English expression dating from about 1670, meaning a shilling.

66. **Ho'penny.** An English–Scottish border counties' collo-
    quialism for halfpenny.
67. **Imperial.** A coin struck in Lombardy at the same time as
    and equivalent to the *denier* (see 30, 34–5, 48).
68. **Joachimsthaler** or **joachimsdaler.** With the renaissance of
    art, letters, and trends in central Europe there developed
    a need for a more universally acceptable coinage and, in
    1519, the proprietor of St. Joachimstal's silver mine in a
    Bohemian valley (*thal* or *dale* meaning "dale" or "valley"),
    minted a large and heavy silver coin called a *joachimsthaler*.
    The introduction of this coin did not immediately result
    in a change in the existing system of account but, in
    course of time, other and somewhat similar coins were
    minted and called *thaler* in German-speaking parts of
    Europe, as *daalder* in Holland, and *daler* in Sweden. A
    corruption of *thaler* was adopted in the form *dollar* and
    piastro (Fig. 6 and also Nos. 37, 42).
69. **Kronor.** A unit of monetary value in circulation in Denmark,
    Norway, and Sweden, but not of the same value in each
    country. The abbreviation in the first two countries is *kr.*
    and in the third *Kr.* The English translation is *crowns*.
70. **L** or **£.** Both abbreviations are used to indicate *lira* or *lire*,
    an Italian monetary unit. The name is derived from the
    Latin *libra* meaning "pound" (originally the weight of a
    pound of silver).
71. **£.** The abbreviation used in Britain to indicate pound(s)
    sterling and at one time the monetary value of a pound
    of silver (see 34, 44, 48).
72. **Libra.** See 70–1. The French equivalent is *livre*.
73. **Lira.** See 70.
74. **Mag** or **magpie.** A colloquialism for an English halfpenny,
    used from the eighteenth century.
75. **Maggie Rabb** or **robb.** A Scottish colloquialism for a bogus
    halfpenny in use during the latter part of the nineteenth
    century. Also a slang expression for a tip given to servants.
76. **Manah** or **mina.** An early Babylonian and Greek standard of

FIG. 6. These coins are *joachimsthaler*, the large and heavy silver coins originally minted in Bohemia from about 1519 onwards from metal mined locally. Later shortened to *thaler* in German-speaking countries, the *joachimsthaler* inspired the *daalder* of Holland, the *daler* of Sweden, and the *dollar* of the United States of America and other countries.

weight equivalent to one-sixtieth part of a *talent*, a monetary value.

77. **Mark.** A unit of monetary value in Finland, West Germany, etc. Abbreviation: Mk. (see 36).

78. **Maundy money.** Money given by tradition to the poor on Maundy Thursday, the Thursday preceding Easter's Good Friday, by the royal almoner of Westminster Abbey. This custom is a symbolic commemoration of Christ washing the feet of his disciples.

79. **Mint.** A place where coins are minted or made, usually under state authority. There is a legend that the first state mint was established by King Candaules (Sadyattes) in Asia Minor, but it is more likely to have been under King Gyges, during the seventh century B.C.

80. **Mint condition.** A coin or a postage stamp in a condition as good as when it was made.

81. **Mint mark.** A mark on a coin to indicate where it was minted. The mark usually is to be found on the obverse (i.e. head) side, either above the head or in a small space beneath the line of the subject.

82. **Money.** A simple definition is: any material that by agreement serves as a common medium of exchange and as a measure of value in trade and business. Commonly, the term includes circulating paper money, coins, and demand deposits (i.e. current account deposits) in banks and saving institutions; in fact, money in this simplified definition is exemplified by a material, either at hand or quickly obtained, for use as a common medium of exchange.

83. **Money, Near.** There is much discussion as to the desirable definition of this term which, according to one authority, embraces certain types of liquid assets including time deposits, short-term government obligations, and liquid assets which are not immediately usable like money but which possess some of the important characteristics of money and have significant effects on the working of the

monetary system. The book, published in 1963 by the Governors of the Federal Reserve System of the U.S.A., and entitled *The Federal Reserve System*, states (pp. 6–8): "Commercial banks also hold savings and other time deposits on which an interest return is paid. These deposits are one of the so-called near-moneys shown on the chart." The chart shows:

1. Time and savings deposits at commercial banks.
2. Savings and loan shares.
3. Deposits in mutual savings banks.
4. Short-term U.S. Government securities.

The book goes on to state:

"Savings and time deposits at banks differ importantly from demand deposits. They are not transferable by check. While convertible into demand deposits or currency, savings deposits of individuals are subject to prior notice of conversion. In practice, however, they may generally be withdrawn on request. Other time deposits are not payable before maturity except in emergencies. Thus savings and time deposits, while serving a store-of-value function, are not in themselves means of payment; only currency and demand deposits serve in this active monetary role.

"In addition to time and savings deposits in commercial banks, there are other interest-bearing assets that serve a store-of-value function and that can be turned into money with little inconvenience and little or no risk of loss in value. Such assets include deposits in mutual savings banks, shares in savings and loan associations, short-term U.S. Government securities, and U.S. Government savings bonds.

"For many years now, individuals and businesses have shown a growing preference for near-moneys. But there are limits on the extent to which people can reduce their money balances in favour of other assets. The growing volume of transactions in an expanding economy necessarily requires the ready availability of funds in checking accounts or of hand-to-hand currency."

84. **Money of account.** Money not available in a discrete coinage, but expressed in accepted units.

85. **New penny decimal system.** The decimal currency system proposed for the United Kingdom and presented by the Government for the approval of Parliament in December 1966. The Chancellor of the Exchequer had announced in the House of Commons, in March 1966, that the Government would seek agreement to the adoption of a decimal currency system throughout the country in February 1971. The system comprised retention of the £ as the major unit of currency and its division into 100 minor units called pennies (Fig. 7).

86. **Non-commodity money.** This is money based on a paper standard. Commodity money is based on a gold standard (see 53).

87. **Numismatics.** The study of coins and medals established by law.

88. **Pence** or **pennies.** The plural of penny. Commonly used to indicate value, as in *threepence*, *sixpence*, or as an indefinite number, as in the sentences, "It costs only a few pence" or ". . . pennies".

89. **Penning.** A Dutch coin.

90. **Penny.** A British bronze coin. Abbreviation: 1*d*. Twelve pence (12*d*.) have a value equal to one shilling (1*s*.); and 240*d*. have a value equal to one pound sterling (£1) (see 44). King Offa of Mercia (757–96) was the first to introduce the minting of silver pennies as a replacement for the Anglo-Saxon *denarius*, or *deniers*, made popular by Charlemagne (see 30, 34–5, 48), although the abbreviation *D*. or *d*. was retained. King David I of Scotland (1124–53) introduced a silver *penny* in his country similar to that minted

BRONZE (Plain Edge)

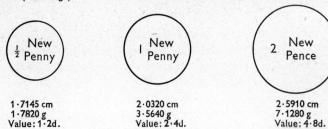

1·7145 cm
1·7820 g
Value: 1·2d.

2·0320 cm
3·5640 g
Value: 2·4d.

2·5910 cm
7·1280 g
Value: 4·8d.

CUPRO–NICKEL (Milled Edge)

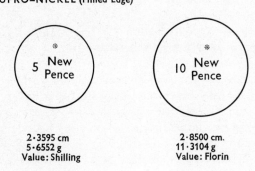

2·3595 cm
5·6552 g
Value: Shilling

2·8500 cm.
11·3104 g
Value: Florin

CUPRO–NICKEL (Plain Edge)

3 cm
13·5 g
Value: 10s

FIG. 7. Here are details of the composition, size, and weight of the British decimal currency that will be issued from February 1971. The 5d. and 10d. pieces will be the same size, weight, metal content, and value as the present 1s. and 2s. coins, though of different design. The other four coins will be of a different size, weight, and value from the coins decimalisation will replace. Although many financial experts were in favour of a 10s. unit, Parliament enforced a system retaining the pound sterling (£1) as the monetary unit.

by King Stephen of England (1135–54). In the reign of King Alexander III of Scotland (1249–86) the expression first appeared, but the coins were later called *sterlings*. In 1257 King Henry III of England (1216–72) struck a gold *penny* valued at 20 silver pennies and, later, at 24. The first English copper *penny* was struck in 1601 during the reign of Queen Elizabeth I (1558–1603). *Penny* is derived from the Anglo–Saxon word *pening*, being similar to the Swedish *penning*, meaning coin, and the German *pfennig*.

91. **Penny decimal system.** See 85.

92. **Penny, American.** A colloquialism for one cent, a one-hundredth part of a dollar. Abbreviation: c.

93. **Peseta.** A Spanish coin.

94. **Peso.** A coin of Spanish antecedents used in South American countries, originally the Spanish equivalent of a dollar.

95. **Petty denier.** See 30, 34–5, 48.

96. **Peter's penny.** A tax at one time levied on every household as a tribute to the Pope.

97. **Piastro.** The Spanish dollar or silver *peso*. Also a Turkish coin (see 68, 94).

98. **Pfennig.** A German coin of value one-hundredth part of a Deutschmark (see 36).

99. **Quid.** A colloquialism for one pound or twenty shillings sterling.

100. **Real.** A Spanish coin issued about the middle of the sixteenth century and worth one-eighth of a *peso*. The expression *pieces of eight* was derived from the markings on the *peso*, one side of which had an armourial shield with the figure VIII (see 42, 94, 97).

101. **Rial.** An Iranian unit of monetary value.

102. **Rupee.** An Indian unit of monetary value.

103. **Schilling.** An Austrian coin. Abbreviation: S.

104. **Shilling.** A British silver or cupro–nickel coin. Abbreviation: *s*. Twenty shillings have the value of one pound (£1) sterling, and twelve pence have the value of one shilling (1*s*.). The name *shilling* is derived from a medieval record

which translated *solidus*—a Roman gold coin—as
schilling or *shilling*. A *shilling* appears as a money of
account in Anglo-Saxon laws (see 7, 34). The first
English shilling was struck in 1504 as part of the third
coinage of King Henry VII (1485–1509) (see Fig. 5).

105. **Sixpence.** A British silver or cupro–nickel coin with a value
of six pence. The first coin was struck in the year 1551,
during the reign of King Edward VI (1547–53) (see Fig. 5).

106. **Skins.** Skins were used as money in many parts of the world.
In some of the islands in the Pacific Ocean skins were used
for this purpose as recently as the 1940's (see section 1.2).

107. **Smasher.** A nineteenth-century slang expression for bad or
counterfeit money.

108. **Solidus.** A gold coin minted by the Romans which gave its
name to a coin minted by Constantine the Great and then
known as the *bezant* or *byzant* (see 7, 30, 34–5, 48, 90, 104).

109. **Sovereign.** A British gold coin with a value of one pound (£1)
sterling when the United Kingdom monetary values were
on a par with the gold standard. The first *sovereign* was
struck in 1817. British gold coins disappeared from circulation in 1914 when Treasury notes were issued instead.
Between 1925 and 1931 there was a brief return to the
gold standard, but not to the use of sovereigns as currency.

110. **Sovereign, Five.** Five-sovereign pieces were struck in 1887
but ceased to circulate in 1914.

111. **Sovereign, Half.** Half-sovereigns of gold were struck first in
1817 but disappeared from circulation in 1914.

112. **Sterling.** Used in association with British monetary units
this expression indicates a standard of value or purity
and is derived from *esterling* (see 44).

113. **Struck.** When a coin of new value is made for the first time,
it is said to be *struck*. The term is a survival from the days
when coins were made by striking pieces of metal with a
punch or die (Fig. 8).

114. **Tanner.** A colloquialism for *sixpence* derived from the gipsy
expression *tano* meaning "small" or "little". A gipsy

fortune-teller customarily asks clients to "cross the gipsy's palm with silver, for good luck", and obviously expects something larger than what was once the smallest silver coin, a threepenny piece, hence the implication that a sixpence also is "little" (see 105).

115. **Thaler.** This was the generic ancestor of many continental European countries' coinage and had a popularity lasting four centuries (see 37, 68).

FIG. 8. This old Swedish woodcut illustrates the literal meaning of "striking" a coin. This quaint glimpse of sixteenth-century minting is taken from *Historia*, a book by the Swedish historian Olaus Magnus.

116. **Threepenny piece.** A British coin with a value of threepence. Originally made of silver, small and round, it was withdrawn from circulation in the mid-twentieth century and replaced by a twelve-sided brass coin (see Fig. 5).

The above is not intended as an exhaustive listing of coins, abbreviations and expressions, monetary history, and practice, but only as a brief outline for the information of readers who may have experienced difficulty in tracing sources of adequate information.

It is noteworthy that in addition to the cumbersome nature of Britain's currency compared with decimal concepts, the use of names such as *half-crown* and *florin* give no immediate indication of the value of the coin, with the result that people who are not familiar with British currency are obliged to memorise names and values in a way that is not so usual with respect to many other countries' monetary systems. The British custom may be quaint, but it is also immensely confusing or, to be blunt, a rank nuisance for many foreign customers for British goods and services, and for visitors to the United Kingdom.

Whilst many of the world's monetary systems are based on both the decimal notation *and* a binary arrangement of names for coins, Britain's system has been made up of a string of names of which about one-third fail to indicate the value in terms of pence, shillings, and parts of a pound. The plethora of abbreviations in general use adds to the confusion, as the following indicates:

1. A halfpenny — equals $\frac{1}{2}d$. — or £–/–/–$\frac{1}{2}$ or –/–$\frac{1}{2}$
2. A penny — equals $1d$. — or £–/–/1 or –/1
3. A threepenny piece — equals $3d$. — or £–/–/3 or –/3
4. A sixpence — equals $6d$. — or £–/–/6 or –/6
5. A shilling — equals $1s$. — or £–/1/– or 1/–
6. A florin — equals $2s$. — or £–/2/– or 2/–
7. A half-crown — equals $2s$. $6d$. — or £–/2/6 or 2/6
8. A pound — equals £1. $0s$. $0d$. or £1/–/– or 20s. or 20/–
9. A guinea — equals £1. $1s$. $0d$. or £1/1/– or 1 gn.

To add confusion, the stroke (/) is often replaced by a full-point (.); for example, one pound and five shillings and sixpence halfpenny may be written:

(a) £1. $5s$. $6\frac{1}{2}d$.
(b) £1. 5. $6\frac{1}{2}$.
(c) £1–5–$6\frac{1}{2}$, etc.

Where a stroke is used, as in £–/–/4, a handwritten dash or stroke can easily be so badly formed that the amount reads as

£7 7 4, or as £– 4/4. Writers are inclined to mix signs as long as a standard is not enforced, so it is hoped the Government Committee on Decimal Currency will extend its work to include recommendations on how the new currency should be written without risk of ambiguity. For example, should we write £1.50, or £1,50, or £1:50? All three methods are used by continental European countries to mean (in local currency) what is shown here to indicate one pound, decimal point, five, nought.

1.7. The Currency Customs of Other Countries

If we contrast the confusing British currency notations with the established customs of some other countries (Table 1), it will be seen how much time could be saved if British notations were reduced to the same number of standard forms, which would be absolutely specific in meaning. For convenience in making comparisons, a figure of 30 major units and 25 minor units of currency has been shown in all examples, except where—as in the case of Italy and Finland—there is only one unit.

Britain is the last great industrial country in the world to have a non-decimal currency system extending into the 1970's. All continental European countries, North and South America, and most of Asia—including Japan and India—will have benefited for many years from this ingredient of national efficiency and external trade promotion before the first native British bank account is designated in the pound sterling decimal. Australia "went decimal" in 1966, and New Zealand made the change in 1967.

1.8. The Development of Banks and their Influence

When money and valuables had to be safeguarded in the Babylon of 2000 B.C., the favours of the gods were invoked. The temples were both the strong-rooms for the storage of gold and other precious articles and the centres for the negotiation of loans. Promissory notes were inscribed on stone tablets or on sun-baked mud slabs. By 600 B.C. a bank-like institution called Igibi had been

TABLE 1.

| Country | Currency denomination and abbreviation | | Standard written forms |
	Major unit	Minor unit	
Austria	Schilling S	groschen g	S 30,25 *or* S 30 25 g
Belgium	Franc Fr	centime Ct	Fr 30,25 *or* 30 Fr 25 Ct
Denmark	Kronor kr	øre øre	kr 30,25 *or* kr 30 øre 25
Finland	Finmark Fmk Mark mk		30 Fmk *or* 30 mk
France	Nouveau Franc NF	centime Ct	NF 30,25 *or* 30,25 NF
West Germany	Deutschmark DM	pfennig pf	DM 30,25 *or* DM 30 25 pf
Holland	Florin fl	cent Ct	fl 30,25 *or* fl 30 25 Ct
	Guelder Gld		Gld 30,25 *or* Gld 30 25 Ct
Italy	Lira L *or* £		L 30 *or* £30
Norway	Kronor kr	öre öre	kr 30,25 *or* kr 30 öre 25
Portugal	Escudos $	centavo c	30 $25 *or* $30 25 c
Spain	Peseta ptas	centimo c	30.25 ptas
Sweden	Kronor Kr	öre öre	Kr 30:25 *or* Kr 30 25 öre
Switzerland	Franc Fr	centime c	Fr 30,25 *or* Fr 30 25 c
U.S.A.	Dollar $	cent c	$30.25 *or* $30 25 c

established and was an advance on earlier Babylonian institutions in that records were scrupulously kept in writing. Despite the metalworking arts of the ancients the skill of the locksmith did not really develop until much later times.

Grecian banking of 400 B.C. spread out beyond the temples to encompass public bodies and private groups. In the Roman Empire banking was well developed although restricted to the wealthy elite, and the payment of debts through a bank was recognised in law and by A.D. 200 a public register of such transactions was in use.

In the time of Jesus a temple was still a place where the ingredients of banking operations could be found. In St. Matthew's Gospel of the Bible is stated (ch. 21, v. 12): "And Jesus went into the temple of God, and cast out all them that sold and bought in the temple, and overthrew the tables of the moneychangers. . . ."

The gradual decline of the Roman Empire produced a corresponding decline in trade. Banking philosophy stagnated until the Mediterranean trading countries' need of banking services developed, and the great banking families of Lombardy and other Italian states came to prominence.

1.8.1. THE ORIGINS OF MODERN BANKS

Money changers and dealers in bullion laid the foundation of modern banking. From the thirteenth century credit banking gradually took shape, although worked by cumbersome and costly methods; for example, the debtor was obliged to give oral instructions in the presence of witnesses for the transfer of credit to his creditor. As the number of people who could read and write was restricted the word of witnesses was the only way by which traders could prove their discharge of debts. Although the non-negotiable bill of exchange had been established in principle by the year A.D. 1350, its applicability was restricted to people in possession of literate powers; it had to be drawn up preferably in the handwriting of the principal.

As the trade of the Italian republics grew, the failures among private bankers increased. Seaborne trade from Venice and Genoa was ever at the mercy of Mediterranean weather—no better in the twentieth century than in the fourteenth century—but far safer for the mariner of today, with the help of radar and weather forecasting, than it was for the Venetian merchants' small sailing ships.

The knife-edge risks of sea and weather in the fourteenth century, coupled with man's impetuosity, are well illustrated in that most famous of all stories of banking and trade in old Venice—in William Shakespeare's *Merchant of Venice*—although written in the latter part of the sixteenth century.

We are told how Antonio, the merchant of Venice, has spread his risks by dispatching his cargoes in several ships (Act I, sc. 1):

> "I thank my fortune for it,
> My ventures are not in one bottom trusted,
> Nor to one place; nor is my whole estate
> Upon the fortune of this present year:
> Therefore, my merchandise makes me not sad."

And Bassanio seeks a loan from Shylock, the Jewish money lender (Act I, sc. 3):

SHY. Three thousand ducats, for three months, and Antonio bound.

BASS. Your answer to that.

SHY. Antonio is a good man.

BASS. Have you heard any imputation to the contrary?

SHY. Oh, no, no, no, no; my meaning in saying he is a good man is to have you understand me that he is sufficient. Yet his means are in supposition; he hath an argosy bound for Tripolis, another to the Indies; I understand moreover upon the Rialto, he hath a third at Mexico, a fourth for England, and other ventures he hath, squandered abroad. But ships are but boards, sailors but men; there be land-rats and water-rats, land-thieves, and water-thieves,—I mean pirates,—and then there is the peril of waters, winds, and rocks. The man is, notwithstanding, sufficient. Three thousand ducats; I think, I may take his bond."

We need not concern ourselves with Antonio's eventual predicament, nor with the guarantee of a pound of his flesh if he defaulted. But the story reflects the very real losses sustained by Venetian merchants and bankers in the thirteenth and fourteenth centuries. By the year 1356 the position was so depressing that a national bank was proposed. But nothing was done for another 200 years. Although regarded as an abuse, bankers had for long allowed their customers to overdraw accounts, with the result than an ever-increasing number of private banks failed, and the only survivors were those so wealthy that they could ride over the insolvency of customers; these were banks owned by families like the Medicis.

By 1584 a body of opinion in favour of public banking had been successful in establishing the Banca della Piazza di Rialto. Its charter decreed that it should receive deposits in coinage, transfer amounts from one account to another, and pay bills of exchange. Services were to be free and a charge on the state. But the bank soon departed from its charter, lent money to the Government, and got into difficulties. It had established for the first time some novel principles, however.*

A new attempt to put these methods into operation was tried in 1619 when the Government's creditors agreed to accept payment in the form of credit from the newly established Banca Giro, which adhered more strictly to its charter. This proved more successful, and in 1638 the two public banks were amalgamated, and continued in business until 1806.

The Bank of Amsterdam was founded in Holland in 1609 with aims similar to the Banca della Piazza di Rialto.

Before the sixteenth century a document corresponding to the modern bank cheque was scarcely known, but as the art of reading and writing extended beyond the confines of royal courts, the homes of the wealthy and powerful, religious foundations, and banks, the legal document of negotiability was gradually established.

Seventeenth-century English goldsmiths were the ancestors of British banks. The written receipts issued to customers by the goldsmiths when they accepted for storage the valuables deposited by customers, were increasingly accepted in business transactions in place of coinage, and these receipts began to assume the importance eventually taken by the first English bank-notes.

* See p. 105.

The bank-note was a Swedish invention. In the year 1661 the Palmstruch Bank in Stockholm issued the first bank-note (Fig. 9) and, incidentally, opened the way to greater criminal activity in the counterfeiting of money. Figure 10 illustrates the world's first recorded forged bank-note, which appeared in 1662. But in

FIG. 9. Europe's first paper money was issued in 1661 by the Bank of Stockholm on the initiative of Johan Palmstruch. This particular bank-note, issued in 1662, had a value of 5 daler *kopparmynt* (copper money). Palmstruch was a native of Riga, then part of Sweden.

countries like Sweden, where the coinage was often cumbersome and heavy, the bank-note was quickly recognised as a far more negotiable type of money. Figure 11 illustrates one of the alternatives to paper money—a 2-daler coin, or piece of *plate money*, comprising a solid slab of copper approximately 0.5 inch thick and measuring 6.6 by 6.6 inches. It was minted in the Swedish town of Avesta in 1716 and, in weight, would have been heavy enough to dissuade any grab-and-run thief. This was one of the smaller pieces of *plate money*, of which considerable quantities were made in addition to more conventional coins.

The Royal Bank of Sweden was founded in 1668 and now is the oldest surviving banking house in the world. Private banking did not commence until about 1830, and joint stock commercial banking started some 34 years later.

1.8.2. THE FOUNDATION OF THE BANKS OF ENGLAND AND SCOTLAND

Following the national financial difficulties resulting from the abdication of King James II and the military and civil disturbances towards the end of the seventeenth century, the Bank of England was established and incorporated in 1694.

The Bank of Scotland was established in 1695 and the Royal Bank of Scotland in 1727. The British Linen Bank was founded in 1744.

The English private banks were the successors of the City of London goldsmiths whose notes, given in exchange for deposits of gold and bullion, became negotiable money. These banks issued their own notes from about 1750 but, from 1770, they increasingly accepted Bank of England notes, and in 1883 these were legalised by Parliament as currency of the realm. The country's gold, not in circulation for some time prior to this, had increasingly been accumulated in the vaults of the Bank of England. The principle of a promise to pay the bearer of a note a certain amount of money on demand, although the amount might not actually be available when the note was issued, dates from the practices of the City goldsmiths who raised loans to meet their current commitments.

The first American commercial bank was opened in 1762, about a century after British colonists in Massachusetts started to mint silver shillings. Although the British banking system was projected as the ideal pattern for every colonial possession and protectorate to copy and, as a result, was a prime influence in the moulding of banking systems and customs in English-speaking countries, a big organisational difference developed between American and British banking progress. This was the strict control in America on the proliferation of branches of banking houses. As it became

FIG. 10. Criminals took little time to find how easily bank-notes could be copied. This forgery of a Palmstruch bank-note had a "value" of 1000 daler *kopparmynt* and was made in 1662. It is the earliest forged bank-note in existence.

almost easier to start a new banking house than to start a branch of an existing bank, there is no American equivalent of the British "Big Five" banking houses with their thousands of branches scattered throughout the towns and villages of the United Kingdom. Another difference—which immensely complicates transactions—is that cheques issued by banks in one state are not

Fig. 11. The last three illustrations may give an impression of unreasonable prominence of things Swedish. But in view of that country's record of financial institution initiative (including in modern times one of the most successful post office giros of all), the emphasis is entirely justified. From the late sixteenth century Swedish coins were, for a time, the largest and heaviest in the world. A 10-daler coin measuring 1 by 2 feet and weighing 40 pounds looked much like this "plate-money" 2-daler piece minted in Avesta in 1716 during the reign of King Charles XII of Sweden. The seemingly wasteful use of copper was due to Sweden's wealth of this metal, mined at Falun in central northern Sweden where, at one period, over 20 per cent of the world's copper originated. The mine is still owned by Stora Kopparbergs Bergslag, which has the distinction of being the world's first limited liability company, with a charter dating from 1347.

always recognised in other states. The world has grown so accustomed to "dollar diplomacy" that few people outside North America—and only narrow sections within its frontiers—have paused to consider the effectiveness of American banking methods, which are now exhibiting signs of acute mechanical strain.

Although America ceased to be a British colony in the latter part of the eighteenth century, links with British banking practice continued to be strengthened as a result of the emigration to America of many young Scottish bankmen from about 1836 onwards.

By 1830 the British banking system of the twentieth century was starting to take shape, and transfers by cheque were assuming a prominent part in business transactions. Indeed, it has been claimed that one of the distinguishing characteristics of the history of banking in Britain and the Commonwealth was the early development of the use of cheques as a means of transferring bank deposits. A cheque is a form of bill of exchange payable on demand, but not of itself money, although of prime importance in providing for the liquidity (i.e. ease in transfer) of money held as a bank deposit.

Since the outset of the First World War gold coins have been out of circulation in the United Kingdom. This position exists globally.

1.9.   Monetary Trends in a Computer-assisted Environment

Britain's reaction to computerised systems has not been as rapid as in countries such as Germany and the United States of America, but the speed of change has noticeably increased with the establishment of a home-based computer industry and the promise it has given for modernisation of a broad spectrum of financial and economic institutions, business, and industrial methods, and the greater prospect thereby engendered of stabilising the nation's economy. Among the more urgent innovations that would be mutually helpful towards this end were the introduction of a National Giro and the change to decimal currency.

More people than ever before have been earning more money

than ever before. This trend—started soon after the Second World War—shows no sign of abating. To avoid inflation and the risk that the more money earned will have a decreasing purchasing power, it is essential that money should be engineered to produce the maximum attainable efficiency in the production of goods and services, civil engineering works, and manufactures of all kinds. This entails the revision of banking methods and changes to make money more perfect in its purchasing power. As the economic system involves the exchange of goods, services, and securities (i.e. promises to pay), with the help of money which, apart from gold, is largely in the form of special types of security such as bank-notes and demand deposits at banks, it follows that any device which can improve the efficiency and lower the cost of transferring deposits (held in either public or private institutions) is likely to be of great value to the economic growth of the country. For this reason alone a giro system is worth establishing. Another major reason is that a giro system can extend the use of public and private bank deposits and can be engineered to take the full advantage of the automated handling methods provided by computer techniques, thereby making monetary processes far less dependent than in the past upon the vagaries of bank employee structure and the multitude of ponderous and individualistic accountancy and handling methods of the bulk of smaller firms, and upon the domestic user.

The British banker's stock reply for many years to every suggestion that banking in the United Kingdom would be better organised if the continental trend of establishing a giro were followed, was that the British joint stock banks have made a special point of catering for the chequing needs of small account holders, and that continental banks had neglected to do so. In retrospect, this argument suggests that British banks took a wrong turning many years ago and ever since have been putting a brave face on the task of catering for a relatively unprofitable class of account holder. The result has been that, in the recent years of steeply rising costs, the burden of catering for the needs of smaller account holders has been more than the banks should have shouldered. On 23 November 1957 one of *The Economist's* experts wrote:

"But it may reasonably be claimed that since the postal cheque service provides the simplest ingredients of a banking service virtually for nothing and that since these particular services are ones that the banking services in Britain, for example, find particularly expensive (and cannot be made to bear their full cost), the co-existence of the postal transfer service with the commercial banks in many European countries is a good thing for both, and for the customer. There is a real distinction between a banking service and a transfer service, and those in Britain who have been exercised about the need for a cheap banking service have rather confused the two. It is a transfer service, plus the ability to cash cheques, that the small banking customer needs, and the continental post cheque service illustrates the technical means by which such a service can be provided cheaply and efficiently."

To those British bankers who have angrily damned the author for "having stirred up the sleeping dogs of giro" it has been pointed out that both British and continental commercial banking institutions developed from broadly the same roots; and that, despite the success of continental post office giros, the banks of Switzerland, Sweden, France, etc., seem to be quite profitable and with material standards quite as good as those of British banks. Moreover, they seem to have escaped many of the staffing problems and the controversy of opening and closing hours which in recent years have so much troubled the British banking scene. In continental banks it is far less usual than in Britain to have to queue at the counter for attention or to be told by the bank clerk to come back at some other time because he is currently too busy to do other than attend to the cheque and deposit needs of customers. Some British banks are beginning to welcome the introduction of a post office giro because they are starting to realise that its efficiency will not only produce greater savings and therefore more surplus money for investment, but that giroists will eventually cream off from their giro deposits any surplus money and the banks will then be even more involved as investment counsellors.

Writing in *The Banker* of October 1959, Professor F. W. Paish observed:

"In conclusion, it may be noted that there is one recommendation in the [Radcliffe] Report which, if adopted on a large scale, might well do more to increase the liquidity of the system than many of the other factors to which the Committee draws attention. This is the institution of a 'giro' system, possibly by the Post Office in co-operation with the banks, which would accept interest-free deposits, to be freely transferable to other 'giro' accounts throughout the country on the instructions, usually written, of the owner. Although part of the rise in 'giro' accounts would no doubt be offset by a reduction in existing forms of money, the final effect would almost certainly be a net addition to the existing stock of media of exchange; and if this addition turned out to be large, its effect would be equivalent to that of the creation of a large additional amount of existing types of money."

In the following chapter we shall see how Britain's economy has been dragged down by the long retention of:

1. Banking methods incompatible with contemporary needs.
2. Post Office money transmission systems which have been archaic and cumbersome compared with those of the rest of western Europe.
3. Monetary methods which discouraged business expansion.
4. Currency and commercial methods which ought to have passed away with the quill pen.
5. Customs and ideas "truly British" which may be quaint and dear to the heart of emotional nationalism, but are murderous to the nation's economy.
6. Commercial customs which took no account of the highly effective facilities used for home and export marketing by many of Britain's principal trading competitors.

CHAPTER 2

The Cost of Using Money

2.1. Monetary System Efficiency

When buying a house or a flat for the first time many people are astonished to find how much the legal charges add to the cost of their purchase. If these same people were entirely logical in their attitudes they would long ago have complained equally about the cost of using a monetary system which, in one year, may cost them as much as the conveyancing fees for their house.

Money in its many forms is an inescapable and universal characteristic of everyday life. In a perfect world the cost of a monetary transaction would be the principal and nothing more. But in practice, a transaction is composed of the principal and the cost of the transaction. In Britain it has been customary for the cost of the transaction to be proportionately greater the smaller the principal, so that the smaller the amount the less economical it is to transfer. As it is unprofitable for a creditor to chase a debtor for a small amount, the tendency has been to up-grade prices to allow a margin for debt-collection contingencies. If this fact is coupled with the tendency to add the cost of transfer to the principal when estimating the cost of a transaction it will be seen there is a natural disinclination to keep costs of goods and services as low as they might be if the costs of operating the monetary system were negligible. Moreover, it is a bad moral principle and has the effect of suggesting that because small debts are unprofitable to chase, the creditor might be encouraged to forget he has not been paid.

If a monetary system is to work well it is necessary to study the requirements of the system in terms of its functions. By this means it is possible in a climate where speed, cost minimisation, and safety are salient factors, to establish conditions for performance optimisation.

An examination of the functions of money given in section 1.3. indicates that common factors of importance are:

1. Efficiency in conversion from one monetary form to another.
2. Efficiency in transfer of money in one form or another.

The desirable characteristics are conveniently illustrated by an analogy, with the petrol used to power an internal combustion engine.

2.1.1.   AN ANALOGY BETWEEN MONEY AND PETROL

It has often been said that money is power. Let us liken money to the petrol used to power an engine which, in turn, powers a car. The required end-product is movement of the car as a result of the petrol powering the engine which drives the wheels.

If both the petrol and the engine are 100 per cent perfect, both are 100 per cent efficient and there is no wastage. But in practice the conversion of petrol into power in the combustion chambers of the engine results in by-products such as heat, carbon and other chemicals, water vapour, and exhaust gases. The transfer of power from the reciprocating motion of the pistons and connecting-rods to the rotary motion of the crankshaft produces friction in the bearings and also air-friction; in addition, the engine consumes some of its own energy in compressing the petroleum gas in the cylinders, operating the gas-inlet and exhaust valves, providing an electrical spark to ignite the gas-mixture, and in sucking the petroleum-gas and air mixture into the combustion chambers, etc.

To obtain the best efficiency from the petrol it must be made as pure as necessary for the conditions under which it is to be burned. Engine efficiency must also be optimised; e.g. bearing and thrust points must be eliminated or made as frictionless as economically possible.

By analogy, money is most efficiently applied when freed of imperfections such as clogging paperwork and processing costs (i.e. by-products), and of handling operations (i.e. friction points). As British monetary conversion and transfer methods have developed out of custom and tradition, there is much to be gained from replanning them to take fullest advantage of electronically controlled computer methods and modern management accountancy techniques. When monetary transactions are thus replanned they will start quickly and effortlessly and, like a clean petrol-powered engine, will run through to completion with efficiency, speed, safety, and economy.

Perfect money is a perfect form of purchasing power—a level to which, for short periods, gold can attain. But today the main forms of money are only near-perfect—or only relatively liquid—securities (i.e. promises to pay by the banks when accepting deposits and promises to pay by the Bank of England on the face value of their bank-notes). Securities classifiable as money must be exchangeable for goods, services, or other securities without delay or paraphernalia; if these conditions are met, the money is said to be highly liquid, and the more liquid it is the nearer it comes to being perfect money. "Near-money" does not include cash deposits (current accounts in banks), but is the name given to time deposits and other assets serving a store-of-value function that are not immediately realisable and therefore do not qualify as "highly liquid" (see section 1.6, No. 83).

A fuller understanding of the defects in the monetary system, to which we have for so long been accustomed that their very familiarity has made us largely blind to its weaknesses, will give a better impression of what a giro has to offer.

2.2. Popular Types of Money

The most popular types of money in everyday use by the majority of the population are:

1. Bank-notes.
2. Coins.
3. Private and public bank deposits as non-interest bearing current accounts.

The mechanics of handling are engineered by a variety of forms which, in effect, are bills of exchange—not themselves money—and act like catalysts. These are:

(a) Commercial bank cheques.
(b) Commercial bank credit transfer forms.
(c) Post Office money orders.
(d) Post Office postal orders.
(e) Post Office Savings Bank warrants.
(f) Trustee Savings Bank cheques.
(g) Credit cards.
(h) Giro transfer forms.

Some authorities prefer to regard Trustee Savings Bank cheques as being part of a system that is more near-money in character than a commercial bank current account. This is true in that a trustee savings bank account holder's deposit has to fulfil certain conditions which have the effect of preventing all his assets from being entirely liquid.

A survey of the convenience and applicability of these popular types of money and the operational mechanics must take into consideration their acceptability in an age when speed, security, impact, transmission efficiency, banking, and handling capability are all of far greater importance than, say, a quarter of a century ago. Essentials that will help us to decide whether one type of money and its processing methods are preferable to another type are:

1. The efficiency of convertability from one type of money to another.
2. The efficiency of transfer from one person to another.
3. Its resistance to criminal misuse and to destruction.
4. Loss recovery capability.

5. Handling convenience.
6. Computer system compatibility.
7. Aesthetic and sentimental appeal.
8. National economic advantage.
9. International compatibility.

2.2.1. CASH COMPRISING BANK-NOTES AND COINS

Cash is the most liquid of all types of money in general use and therefore the most widely acceptable in exchange, but is itself not commendable because of the ease with which it can be destroyed by fire and corrosives. It is easily stolen or lost and costly to safe-guard. Bank-notes are difficult to count quickly when in quantity, and coins—being round and fairly smooth—easily slip between the fingers in hand-to-hand transactions, roll away, and are frequently difficult to recover. Crisp new bank-notes, gaily patterned with designs supposed to discourage counterfeiters, are as aesthetically attractive as gleaming coins newly minted but, in handling by the public, bank-notes are easily torn, soiled, and become carriers of infection. Coins pick up dirt (not always obvious unless examined in a germ-culture laboratory), are often used for purposes other than as money and so tend to wear prematurely or are bent out of shape. As a result of the vast increase in the use of coin-operated machines to dispense goods and services or to measure amounts—as in the case of coin-in-the-slot domestic gas and electricity meters—there are alternative gluts and shortages of some values of coin and, to meet the requirements of these special applications, an artificial demand is created. It would appear that national economy would be better served if coins were not used as mechanical devices to counter-balance slotmeter mechanisms which, in food and gaming mach-ines, public telephone kiosks, parking meters, ticket dispensers, etc., are ever the bait for thieves. The rapidly increasing popu-larity of automatic vending machines seems to call for the production of a system of nationally approved plastic tokens which could easily and cheaply be made with, for example, a variety of crime-proof magnetic codes which would be expended after the token had performed its function in motivating the slotmeter. The alternative to this is the increasing isolation for long periods of a considerable amount of the nation's coinage.

The efficiency of cash conversion to other types of money and its transfer from one person to another is practically 100 per cent if one disregards the intrinsic inconvenience of cash-handling, the time consumed in counting it, and its storage; fireproof safes, money-boxes, cash-bags, and purses are all an added expense.

Cash is the criminal's greatest inducement, as is evidenced by the frequent press reports of attacks on wage-clerks collecting money from the banks, the street-corner-thug who lies in wait for a shopkeeper on his way to a bank's night safe with the day's takings, and the cat-burglar who knows that many housewives keep a small store of money in the bedroom dressing-table drawers or wardrobe to meet unexpected household bills. Snatch-and-run attacks have proved so profitable that, even if the thug is caught and imprisoned, he frequently returns to this type of crime on release. Despite the employment of armed guards and radio-controlled security vans to protect cash in transit, recent experience has shown that if the likely haul is worth the risks, the scientifically trained and well-equipped criminal is willing to hijack a van in daylight even in central London's busiest streets, and stands a chance of getting away with thousands of pounds in bank-notes and coins. Even the woman shopper's handbag is not immune from petty thieves.

Coin counterfeiters seem to have found that the purchasing power of what has been Britain's largest coin in general circulation —a half-crown— has been too small to make their skill profitable, but they may be having different ideas about decimal coins, the largest of which will have a value of ten shillings (see Fig. 7). Despite great devotion in guarding the secrets of bank-note materials' manufacture, the etching of printing plates (Fig. 12) and the production of special inks, the counterfeiting of bank-notes in recent times has often reached such a degree of near-perfection that only experts can distinguish the genuine from the

FIG. 12. The techniques of bank-note design and production involve a
broad range of scarce skills developed over the last few hundred years
as a means of making forgery difficult. The great problem always is to
make paper money at once economical enough for national monetary
system quantity production, and so difficult to copy that even a scientifically trained syndicate of criminals will not attempt to counterfeit it.
Coins are always made at the Royal Mint, but the Bank of England
orders paper money from firms like Thomas de la Rue, where this photograph of an engraver at work was taken. Although the trend towards a
reduction in public demand for bank-notes will be enhanced by the credit
transfer methods of the National Giro and the joint stock banks' modernisation programmes, the valuable skills of bank-note makers are not
likely to be wasted; if American views on credit and money card development are to be realised without a built-in risk of fraud there will be plenty
of opportunity for engravers like the one shown here to apply their talents.

forged note. In the late 1950's a nation-wide scare followed the
discovery of forged £5 notes in widespread circulation and, in
Essex, a source of possible 10s. bank-note forgeries was discovered,
with the result that Essex housewives were for some weeks

reluctant to accept change containing 10s. notes. During the Second World War the Germans printed many thousands of "Bank of England" notes with a view to circulating them and disrupting Britain's economy; a forgotten cache of these notes was discovered in central Europe during the summer of 1967.

As criminals grow even more scientific in their methods and brazen in their attitudes, the risk of large-scale bank-note counterfeiting will increase unless the public can be persuaded to reduce its demand for paper money. Since 1950, the issue of bank-notes has grown at an annual rate of some £100 million and to satisfy this demand as well as to replace worn-out notes is quite a costly printing operation. Another factor which might encourage criminals is the attempt by the Government to persuade the public to use existing bank-notes for a longer time, instead of persistently asking for crisp and clean new notes. Paper money is so vulnerable to a variety of criminal activities and accidents that it scarcely accords with the needs of the twentieth century. Although coins are less destructible, their weight–size relationship as well as the other disadvantages, make them no more acceptable than bank-notes; moreover, neither are directly compatible with computer operation.

But the use of cash is such an ingrained national habit that despite the advantages of discouraging its continuing use, the chances of a rapid change to private or public bank deposits worked in association with a giro-like system seems a long way off to people without personal experience of continental giros. But even in giro countries there is a growing awareness that the amount of cash in circulation is often too great and that it represents a rather wasteful use of industrially valuable metals. If the trend towards reduction in demand for coins develops, the amount of raw metal used by the Royal Mint (Fig. 13) will gradually decline, or the metal of newly minted coins will be set off against those recalled for melting down. It is true that a certain section of the community will always wish to use cash in transactions; it is that section who find it more convenient to carry on all their

Fig. 13. The raw material for money in Britain is a special grade of high-quality paper and industrially valuable metal such as these ingots of copper being fed into a machine at the Royal Mint. It is ironical that the electronic computers that now are modernising Britain's banking and monetary system rely heavily in their electronic circuits on copper, nickel, zinc, and tin—the four metals used in making coins. But the conversion efficiency of a computer which, despite its size, cost, and gargantuan appetite for work, uses only minute quantities of these valuable metals in comparison with the amount circulating as coins, makes computer construction use of these metals infinitely more economical. When considering the advantages to be gained in other directions by a reduction in public demand for cash, it is necessary to take into account the fact that, during the 1960's, there was in circulation, in the form of coins, some 13 900 tons of cupro–nickel and old silver in the shape of 5s., 2s. 6d., 2s., 1s., 6d., and old 3d. pieces; 4200 tons of brass 3d. pieces; 18 800 tons of bronze and old copper 1d. and ½d. pieces; and several hundred tons of discontinued farthings hoarded by the public for sentimental reasons and as collectors' items.

business affairs in this medium simply because the income tax inspector has greater difficulty in confirming profits.

To sum up, the advantages of bank-notes and coins as money would appear to be balanced by the disadvantages, among which must be included the increasingly acute risk of bodily injury to people known to be carrying, or dealing in, fair amounts of cash (Fig. 14).

2.2.2.   MONEY IN COMMERCIAL BANK CURRENT ACCOUNT DEPOSITS

Money held in the current account of a private or commercial bank, or Post Office Savings Bank, is available on demand and therefore is as liquid as cash. Although bank failures occur from time to time and unusual circumstances develop as when, in 1965, a Hong Kong bank ran so short of ready cash that the demands of customers could not be met until supplies of bank-notes were specially flown out from London, large-scale banking failures— either temporary or permanent—are negligible thanks to the firmly imposed government regulations of most countries.

In Chapter 1 it was said that a high proportion of wage and salary earners have refused payment except in cash because, in their view, payment by cheque and other types of credit transfer would involve them in using a banking system seemingly too exclusive, cumbrous, costly, and complicated.

But to governments, business and professional men, and the "middle classes", the current account bank deposit system has for long seemed commendable as a form of money with a high degree of liquidity.

The difference between these opposing points of view can be bridged by reorganisation of current account methods. This is

FIG. 14. Newspaper announcements like these are typical of a civilisation which has so much lost control of its monetary system that it has become the sport of criminals. The trend towards a reduction in cash-handling encouraged by both the National and Bank Giros is the best way to minimise crime risks.

£52,000 LONDON BANK RAID BY ARMED GAN[G]

COSH BANDIT HIDES IN VAN TO GRAB WAGES

By OUR SCOTLAND YARD CORRESPONDENT

A NEW wage snatch method was used in London yesterday when about £450 was stolen. Mr. Arthur Brown, 54, of Clapham Junction ha[d] been to a branch of the Midland Bank ... e £450.

£5000 GRAB IN PALL MALL

A gang grabbed £5000 wages in Waterloo Place, Pall Mall this afternoon from two employees of he Cleveland Bridge and Engi... ...g Co who were taking the

TRUNCHEON GANG GRABS £5,000 RATES MONEY

COUNCIL VAN ATTACKED IN TRAFF[...]

Window clean-up—Two men posing as window cleaners attacked a Temple Press employee, seizing £5,000 cash—in Bowling Green Lane, Clerkenwell, scene of the £711,000 gold raid.

DAILY TELE[...]

Hold-up in New Ken[t] Road

By JOHN PONDER

Six masked men waving one revolver, rushed two cashiers opening the vaults in a London bank today and stole £52,250.

THE TIME: just after...

'Thuggery'

While detectives dusted finger-prints and examined bullet holes. Barclays' Chief Security Officer, ex-Flying Squad man...

"Ruby" Sparks.

"Observer" reporter; ... up was a typical comm... raid."

The former chief insp... retired from Scotland... 1961, added: "It all ha... suddenly that nobo... appreciated what was g... "The raid was almos...

Key to £44,000

In 20 seconds thieves raided and drove off an immobilised security van in Carlow Street, Camden Town—with £44,000 cash for British Railways wages. The van was found later, locks intact. Someone had a good set of keys, said Security Express.

by the ...n's vans. ... into the ... the bandit ... hid be... using the ...van had

Cosh gang's big pay snatch

About £48,000 wages money was snatched by a cosh gang from The Times building in Printing Hous[e]

RAIDERS using explosive failed to blow open the safe at Kings Langley Post Office during Friday night. But they did succeed in keeping the post office closed on Saturday.

Four men coshed a postman in Basinghall Street, E.C... grabbing mailbags said to hold £8,000 cash.

Beat the Wage Bandits

FOUR men wearing crash helmets and goggles held up a van carrying £5,000 collected for rates and rents when it ...s stopped in a traffic queue at Welling, Kent, last night.

FIG. 14

what the Bank Giro is doing, and what the National Giro has been designed to progress still more. To understand the changes needed it is necessary to look at the mechanics of money transfer in the same way as we have examined the merits of cash.

We will first examine the transfer of money by bank cheque, and then by what is called bank credit transfer.

Note: The flow diagrams illustrating the various transfer methods are drawn with particular reference to the instalment repayments made by a customer of a hire purchase finance house, but the information given is also true for all types of payment by the method illustrated. These diagrams first appeared in an article the author wrote for *Credit*, the quarterly journal of the Finance Houses Association, and comprised part of the information provided for Members of Parliament in advance of the debate in Parliament, on 21 July 1965, which resulted in the decision to establish the National Giro.

1. *Transfer of Money by Bank Cheque* (Fig. 15)

In essence, a cheque is an order written out by an account holder to his bank to make payment from his account, and he can write the cheque so as to have payment made to himself—in the form of cash—or to the institution or person named. The negotiability of the cheque can be limited to the institution or person named or it may be presented for payment at the bank of an institution or person not named by the remitter. When the remitter (i.e. bank account holder or debtor) wishes to limit the cheque so that he can trace the creditor—if necessary—he either issues a cheque preprinted by his bank with crossed lines, or he draws two parallel lines separated by approximately 0.5 inch across the face of the cheque, in a diagonal direction. As a crossed cheque cannot be encashed at a bank, but only paid to the account of the institution or person who presents it at a bank, the remitter has a record available to him of who benefited from his cheque. To

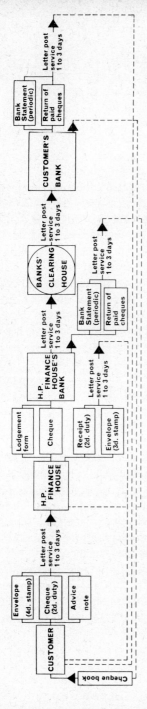

Fig. 15. Payments made by joint stock bank cheque involve both the remitter and the beneficiary in an unreasonable amount of paper-work, provision of stationery, incidental charges, and expenditure of time. What ought to be a simple, straightforward operation between two parties becomes an unreasonably long sequence in which a loss in transit at any stage can cause time-wasting remedial exercises. The remitter—shown in this flow diagram as the customer of a finance house hire purchase service—may have to wait a week or longer to hear that his cheque has safely arrived and, if the finance house requires proof of the creditworthiness of the cheque before they issue a receipt, the remitter may have to wait even longer. If the instalment payment was for £2 or more, the beneficiary is still under an obligation to render a receipt—if required by the remitter to do so—and a stamp duty of 2d. is required. Neither the customer nor the finance house can be absolutely sure of the success of the entire operation until each receives his respective bank's periodic statement of account; if the payment is made just after the last statement was received, the customer–remitter may have to wait a month or longer and the finance house—unless it has paid the bank for a very frequent statement service—may suffer the same delay. The entire transaction suffers from too many handling operations by too many people; too many transfers of pieces of paper between too many addresses and too many delays. The wonder is that the joint stock banks' cheque system served the community well enough for business to survive for so long. But it is a painful experience for any person who has been brought up on monetary transmission methods such as those found in most continental countries.

limit the cheque to payment to a particular account, the remitter writes between the cross-lines "a/c payee", "& Co.", "not negotiable", etc., according to requirements. A cheque can be presented at the bank of a third party if the institution or person nominated on it has endorsed the cheque with its, or his, name on the reverse side, provided the remitter has not limited payment to a particular account by the method mentioned above. The transfer efficiency of a cheque is adequately illustrated in Fig. 15. As the remitter of a cheque is still entitled to demand a receipt, and the beneficiary is not obliged to issue one until he has confirmation that the cheque is creditworthy, it will be seen that several days may elapse before the remitter has proof that he has discharged a debt. If the cheque is lost in transit or is misappropriated, the process is even more involved and inefficient.

The cheque system is susceptible to criminal misuse and much valuable time may be lost in tracing embezzlement or fraud because of the system. Moreover, the handling processes through which a cheque passes are not foolproof, and an account holder may not know he has been robbed until his next periodic statement arrives. A cheque is easily destroyed or lost and—if the latter occurs—it is so unrewarding to try and find the point of loss that it is usually better to cancel the original and to write out a new cheque. The watch for erring cheques puts a heavy strain on bank personnel, and the issue of a replacement doubles the processes for the remitter.

Since a degree of computer-centred accountancy was introduced by the banks in 1960, the bank account holder has found he is obtaining less service and is required by some banks to keep more detailed written records. The introduction of a stubless cheque book is a particular example of the latter complaint. Periodic statement sheets contain far less information, and recently one of the Big Five banks suggested that used cheques would not be returned to account holders. A cheque has computer compatibility only within the banking system and, up to the present, the magnetic-ink character line has been useless in facilitating the account holder's or payee's office records system. Although the

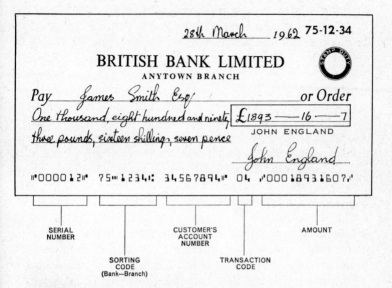

28th March   1962 75-12-34

BRITISH BANK LIMITED
ANYTOWN BRANCH

Pay   James Smith Esq   or Order

One thousand, eight hundred and ninety   £1893 ——— 16 ——— 7

three pounds, sixteen shilling, seven pence

JOHN ENGLAND

John England

⑂000012⑂ 75⑂1234⑂ 34567894⑂ 04 ⑂0001893 1607⑂

SERIAL NUMBER

SORTING CODE
(Bank—Branch)

CUSTOMER'S ACCOUNT NUMBER

TRANSACTION CODE

AMOUNT

FIG. 16. This dummy cheque illustrates the standard of layout agreed by the Committee of London Clearing Banks in 1961. When a bank's customer receives his cheque book he should find pre-encoded in magnetic ink the code line comprising the cheque serial number, the bank and branch sorting code, his own account number, and a transaction code. The amount is added in magnetisable characters after the beneficiary has paid the cheque into his bank. The fact that few banks have adopted this standard in its entirety is a small but significant indication of the banks' individualistic attitudes. Very few banks return cheques to the remitter, after processing, with more than four code groups and some have only three groups. The ink is not magnetised (except for the minute amount caused by the earth's magnetic field) until processed by the electronic sorter–reader, just before passage through the bank computer.

Committee of London Clearing Banks inaugurated in 1962 a magnetic-ink line character standard for cheques (Fig. 16), many banks have not entirely adopted it and even branches within a banking house group have variations.

A good deal of sentiment is attached to the cheque system. This is a legacy from the time when the banks discriminated more than at present in the selection of customers and it was a prestige symbol to be admitted to this clientele. The gift of a cheque could be more of an embarrassment than a blessing if the recipient was outside the class respected by bankers.

The monopolistic servicing of trade accounts, for so long held by the commercial banks, encouraged them to provide facilities which only just commanded the respect of their customers. This had the effect of making inter-bank competition concentrate more on obtaining good new accounts than on stimulating research into banking-system development and the introduction of radically improved management methods; people are by nature nervous of changes affecting monetary institutions and it might not have been politic—unless external pressures forced them—for banks to indulge in massive and what might look like extremely costly and relatively unnecessary changes. But within a few months of Parliament's decision to establish a National Giro the banks announced they had placed orders for millions of pounds worth of computers and ancillary automated handling equipment that would "make their counter facilities competitive with what the National Giro offers". This, perhaps, is one of the most classic examples of how a government-sponsored institution in competition with private enterprise has had the effect of modernising an industry and of encouraging the acceptance of a technology— computers in this case—which had made little headway in sales in the United Kingdom. From the public's point of view this change will be immensely beneficial. Apart from the increase in jobs in a British-based computer industry, the wage-earner's mistrust of banking practices will tend to disappear when bank charges—called by one well-known financial expert, "more of an art then a science"—tend to disappear and the commercial banks align the quality and cost of their services to be fully competitive with what the National Giro offers. The reluctance of the "high majority" of wage and salary earners will tend to soften when the causes of their prejudices against payment by cheque are so effectively removed, and national economic stability will increase when there is less opportunity for thugs to cosh wage-clerks and snatch wage-packets, or to shoot up bank-clerks and innocent bystanders or to ambush post office vansmen handling registered bags containing cash. As the opportunities for organised scientific crime involving bank-notes and coins diminish there will be a corresponding reduction of calls on the police and for hospital and judicial help.

But whilst encouraging wage-earners to accept payment by cheque—and removing cause for antagonism against this system—the banks appear to be trying to encourage continuing expansion in the handling of cash. It was recently announced that an alternative to wage-clerks collecting cash from the banks would be the introduction of a mobile bank to visit factory yards, where the functions of the firm's wages clerk would be taken over by the bank. As this merely transfers responsibility for security from the firm's wages department, with the need for employees to queue up in front of a weather-exposed cash window of a van in what may well be an already overcrowded factory yard, this development seems to be a retrograde step open to opportunities by wage-snatch bandits. The cash-dispenser some banks are installing also appears to be a good way of baiting a trap for the unwary whilst the armed thug lies in wait for a victim.

It is true that the banks are now making preparations for the substitution of alternative methods including account holders' use of magnetic tape in place of written cheques, but there does seem to be little attempt to discourage the use of paper cheques which, in reality, have passed the peak of usefulness in an increasingly mechanised age. Abroad, in giro countries, it is most unusual for bank cheques to be used for the transfer of smallish amounts and a British bank cheque endorsed for payment at a continental giro country's commercial bank is often regarded with surprise if the transfer is for less than about £100. Continental firms transfer such small amounts between themselves by the interlinked post office giro of each country.

The journey made by an American bank *check* is basically similar to its British equivalent, but the large number of banking houses and the strict regulations governing their extension by the opening of new branches, coupled with the immense distances and consequent transit delays and the variable weather conditions, make for even greater problems than in the United Kingdom (Fig. 17).

2. *Transfer of Money by Bank Credit Transfer* (*Bank Giro*)

Bankers have claimed that the Credit Transfer (originally called Traders' Credit Transfer) is the cheapest, speediest, and most efficient of all methods for their account holders to make regular and multiple payments, and that this service is also eminently suited for the payments, for a nominal fee, of the non-banking public. The main benefit of the service is derived by firms and institutions which have to make a large number of regular remittances, such as for the payment of wages and salaries. Instead of preparing a separate cheque for each payment the remitter merely lists in triplicate the payee's name, address, bank branch and code number, and the amount to be transferred. He writes out a credit transfer slip in the name of each payee and sends these, with two copies of the list—usually referred to as a "schedule"—with a cheque to cover the total of all the individual amounts to his bank, keeping the third copy of the schedule for his own records. The entire transaction is then arranged by the banks of the remitter and payees, the former receiving back, in

---

Fig. 17. The journey made by an American bank cheque (*check*) is basically the same as the British equivalent except that both the remitter and the beneficiary are spared the payment of stamp duty. This much-simplified flow diagram gives the impression of greater speed and fewer handling operations, but, in fact, the American cheque transaction is even more complex because of the greater number of banking houses compared with Britain, and the deleterious effect of weather and geography. As will be detailed in a later chapter, the American banking system is approaching blockage due to the difficulty of processing so many millions of cheques. One American expert recently remarked that the flood of cheques had so much increased in the 1960's that the central clearing organisations were "going insane". A potential solution to this problem would be the establishment of state giros on the British model, with each state centre interlinked both for computer operation and facsimile transmission equipment, the latter being used to eliminate inter-state transfer of giro form slips.

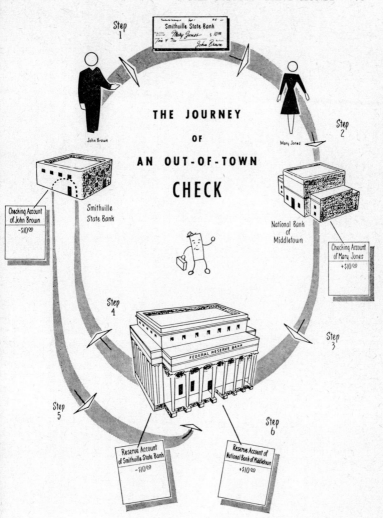

Step 1

Smithville State Bank

Mary Jones $ 10.00

Ten and no/100

John Brown

John Brown

Mary Jones

Step 2

THE JOURNEY
OF
AN OUT-OF-TOWN
CHECK

Checking Account
of John Brown
−$10.00

Smithville
State Bank

National Bank
of
Middletown

Checking Account
of Mary Jones
+$10.00

Step 4

Step 3

FEDERAL RESERVE BANK

Step 5

Step 6

Reserve Account
of Smithville State Bank
−$10.00

Reserve Account of
National Bank of Middletown
+$10.00

Fig. 17

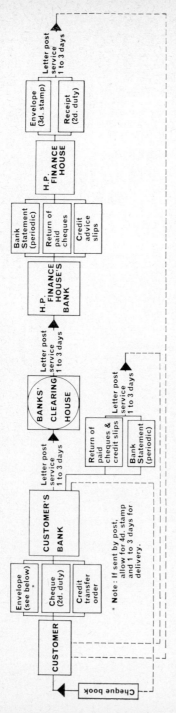

FIG. 18. Payment by bank credit transfer or banker's order is not much less cumbersome than payment by cheque. Few private people have enough payments to benefit from the opportunity to order several payments at once under cover of one cheque. From the payee's position this method is even more unsatisfactory; he has no immediate evidence of payment to his bank account until he receives the periodic statement issued by his bank, accompanied by the credit transfer advice slip(s). The writing of the advice(s) is not infrequently so bad that it is necessary to make inquiries as to the origin and purpose of the remittance. Since March 1967 bank account holders making credit transfers between each other have received a free service with no maximum or minimum limit on the amount transferred, and transfer orders made through a bank by a person with no account to one who has, receives service at a fee of 6d. per transfer. In April 1967 the London Clearing Banks and Scottish Banks announced the introduction of a standard format for the magnetic tape encoding of bank computers, so that customers with extensive business in credit transfers 'and automatic debiting would be able to replace paper vouchers and other paperwork with magnetic tapes that would pass from customers to the bank computer and vice versa. But the smaller users of bank credit transfers will still find their transfers processed by the methods outlined here.

due course, one copy of his schedule as confirmation of the transactions, and the latter the credit transfer notification slip when next their bank sends out periodic statements of account. An alternative system, now under development, uses a magnetically encoded tape in place of the written paperwork schedule supplied by the remitter—a great saving in time when a large number of transfers have to be made (see Fig. 18).

Although this method is an advance on the bank cheque method described earlier, it still has major drawbacks. For example, the beneficiary is unlikely to know that a transfer has been made to his credit until next he receives a bank statement, which may be some weeks unless his banking transactions are large enough for it to be profitable for him to demand a daily statement of account from his bank. There is also the not infrequent problem of deciphering a badly written credit notification slip. An increasing number of firms send invoices with an integrated credit transfer notification slip to encourage debtors to pay through their bank by this method. But until the banks issue a comprehensive directory of account holders' branch code numbers, the system will continue to be limited in scope and appeal.

The risks of criminal interference are slightly less than for the bank-cheque methods described previously. But the risk of destruction of paperwork and postal and other losses is as great, with the added chance of the wrong account being credited as a result of an error in code numbers; and the likelihood that a mistake will not show up until the payee next sees his bank statement. Compared with National Giro facilities, the cost to the bank account holder is greater.

There is evidence that the banks hoped to forestall the development of the National Giro by persuading the public that the giro had nothing to offer that the banks could not do as well, or better, or that the banks were the best nation-wide organisation to operate a giro, but apart from the announcement in March 1967 that the banks would operate a credit transfer service free to their account holders with no lower limit on free transfers (as opposed to the 5s. lower limit imposed by the National Giro

Authority), they cannot improve on the cheapness and speed of service promised by the National Giro which, being part of the Post Office service, is the only organisation recognised for international payment transfers by this method. The Bank Giro or credit transfer service is effectively the same as the Bankgiro operated by, for example, Sweden's commercial banks, although not centralised to the same degree and probably offering only as much appeal as

---

Fig. 19. Payments made by Post Office money or postal orders, savings bank warrant, or periodic payment order are, in general, less prolonged but far more irritating. Although the Post Office has the customer's money at its disposal from the time he purchases a money or postal order until it is cleared by the finance house bank—and the ratio of poundage charged to the value of the order can amount to 10 per cent or more—he is not entitled to any special service or security. Purchasers of postal orders are often justifiably irritated by the thoughtless design of the order, with the very small space for the beneficiary's name marred by wavy coloured lines that make the name difficult to read, and by large round holes placed right over the space. The counterfoil, too, irritates because space is too small to make other than the most abbreviated notes, and the length of the paper is too short to accept standard-distanced punched holes to facilitate storage in a lever-arch file. If some value other than the preprinted denomination has to be transmitted, the extra must be made up by purchasing additional postal orders and duplicating the beneficiary's name, etc., or by fixing postage stamps. But if a postal order is lost in transit, the maximum the remitter can claim is the amount pre-printed on the counterfoil; no allowance is made for stamps added to increase the value. If a postal order is lost and a claim is made against the Post Office they will initiate action only after the remitter has surrendered his only legal proof of purchase—the counterfoil. A money order is obtainable in any amount up to £50 and the minimum poundage charged is 2s. As the remitter is obliged to give the Post Office the beneficiary's name and, to encash the order, the latter must give the remitter's name correctly, there is always risk of endless delays if one has accidentally mis-spelt the other's name. When a postal or money order is lost in transit, the remitter may have to double his outlay and purchase duplicate order(s) whilst the Post Office is tracing the lost remittance, and this frequently embarrasses people living on a tight budget. Until the finance house bank has paid postal orders received into its post office account, and the reference numbers of these have been checked by the authorities, there is no means of knowing whether the postal orders have been earmarked as part of a robbery from, say, a sub-post office. The issue of Post Office Savings Bank warrants is often excruciatingly slow, and regulations for the periodic payments service are almost offensive. Of all British money and credit transfer systems, those of the Post Office have been the most costly and cumbersome, and in need of improvement with a view to wooing the public instead of treating them like servants.

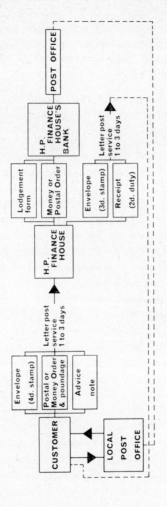

Fig. 19

the Swedish Bankgiro has done in the presence of a very efficiently organised post office giro centred on the Stockholm Post Giro Clearing Centre.

The non-banking British public can obtain service through the bank credit transfer system on payment of a fee of sixpence per transfer.

2.2.3. TRANSFER OF MONEY BY POST OFFICE MONEY AND POSTAL ORDERS, POST OFFICE SAVINGS BANK WARRANTS AND PERIODIC PAYMENTS (Fig. 19)

Britain's money order system was introduced in 1838 and the postal order system in 1881. Both have remained more or less unchanged since and now represent costly and archaic ways of transferring money. Efficiency is stifled by the high cost to the user, excessive paperwork, unreasonable delays, petty restrictions, and poor public relations on the part of the Post Office.

Post Office Savings Bank warrants involve delays which make them an unrealistic way to transfer money. The POSB periodic payments service imposes regulations on the account holder which makes this service analogous with the characteristics of "near-money" instead of one of monetary fluidity. Regulations require the account holder to maintain a "reasonable balance" in his account and the definition of "reasonable" appears to be determined entirely by the Post Office. Further, he is required to pay *annually in advance of receiving service* a fee of one shilling for each payment, and the frequency of periodicity may not exceed one per calendar month. The extraordinary regulations imposed by the Post Office automatically discourages—or makes the use of the service impossible for—weekly wage-earners living on budgets so tight that they can only make weekly payments, such as house rents. *If* one of the objects of the Post Office Savings Bank is to provide a service for lower income groups it is more than time these dictatorial and restricting edicts were amended. The service is uncompetitive with that of commercial banks, except that POSB account holders receive 2.5 per cent interest on each complete pound held in their account per calendar month, and no interest is paid on commercial bank current account deposits.

Post Office monetary transfer methods have in recent years been the target for criminal activity and the stock of postal order forms held by sub-post offices one of the main enticements. These slips of flimsy paper are printed in a variety of denominations and only need the addition of an (easily forged) official rubber-stamped ink mark for authorisation. The cost of guarding and checking orders in advance of sale to the public must be considerable. If a postal or a money order is lost in transit the purchaser may have to make good his loss by purchasing a duplicate to keep to his payment obligations whilst the lost order(s) is being sought, even though he is involved in double the expense. Being printed on easily torn and defaced paper, orders are easily destroyed accidentally or mislaid. The counterfoil is too short to accept punched holes for storage in a standard lever-arch type of file, and the space for entering particulars of the payee and payment are cramped and inadequate (Fig. 20). Neither postal nor money orders are directly compatible with computer use and record-keeping.

Until recent years the postal-order system has been profitable for the Post Office, but money orders have been run at a loss. The following information (Table 2) was taken from *The Post Office Report and Accounts 1965–6*.

As soon as the extremely costly and inefficient money- and postal-order system is allowed to fade out—as the Postmaster-General suggested the latter might do when he spoke in the House of Commons on 20 January 1967—the greater is the chance that Britain might have a single money-order system comparable with and organised on similar lines to the continental giro countries' giro-compatible money-order system. In addition to eliminating the risks to which British money and postal orders are subject, it is both cheaper to the Post Office and to the user to operate. There are, likewise, similar services to the POSB warrant and periodic-payments systems which could, advantageously for all concerned, replace these dreary British methods.

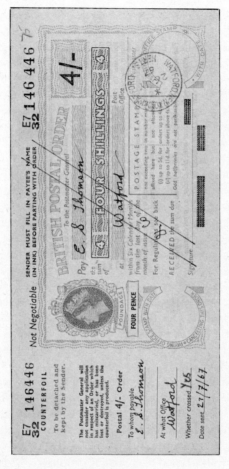

FIG. 20. Oversea readers may not be familiar with British postal orders, of which this is one with a value of 4s. and a poundage charge of 4d. The tear-off counterfoil is separated by a verticle line of perforations. British readers will probably be so familiar with postal orders that they will not have paused to view these scraps of flimsy paper with a proper degree of criticism.

TABLE 2.

	1964–5		1965–6	
	Millions	value (£ million)	Millions	value (£ million)
Money orders issued				
for inland service,	11.5	212.9	11.0	216.9
for overseas service	2.9	16.7	3.0	18.0
Postal orders issued				
at post office counters	643.9	587.0	673.6	634.3
		Loss:		Loss:
Money order poundage	£2.05	−1.5	£1.9	−1.7
Postal order poundage	£9.47	−0.2	£9.98	−0.5

2.2.4.   MONETARY TRANSFER BY TRUSTEE SAVINGS BANK CHEQUE

The characteristics of this service are comparable with those of the commercial bank cheque service except that restrictions placed on account holders have caused some authorities to regard this as a "near-money" service rather than being bracketed with the monetary fluidity characteristics of a current account bank deposit. A trustee savings bank account holder is required to maintain a minimum deposit of £30 in his account in order to qualify for the cheque service. There is usually a handling charge of 1s. per cheque, or 6d. per cheque if drawn to pay cash to self. Alternatively, 10s. worth of free cheques is allowed for each £50 held on account per half-year. There is strong similarity between trustee savings banks and the Post Office Savings Bank, and neither accept commercial accounts.

2.2.5.   MONETARY TRANSFER BY CREDIT CARD

Credit cards are an American-originated method of speeding up the transfer of bank current account deposits. A card enables sellers of goods and services—particularly shop-keepers, hotel proprietors, garage owners, etc.—to accept on trust (or credit) the cheques drawn by the owner of the card up to a certain limit. Cards have no necessary connection with loans to customers of the bank but are simply an assurance to sellers that the debts incurred by the card-holder will be met. The card-holder is trusted by the bank not to abuse the facilities the card allows, such as by overdrawing the amount the card allows him to expend, or the amount of overdraft the bank will allow on his account with them.

A major disadvantage of the system is that the card only commands purchases and services at shops, hotels, etc., that have agreed with the card's issuing authority to collaborate with them. Not a few trading groups find that their paperwork involvement and profit reduction is so great (a percentage on sales turnover is payable to the credit card company) that participation is unprofitable. On the other hand, the card-holder is limited to trading only with shops, etc., within the scheme, and these establishments might not attract his attention if he had a free choice; conversely, the advantages to the shop-keeper, etc., of having a "captive customer" group results in a less competitive spirit and the opportunity for a lowered set of standards. In rural areas many credit card users find so much difficulty that they are obliged to carry cash anyway.

The Multiple Shops Federation announced in July 1966 that their 40 000 member shops would not participate in any credit card scheme. The reason given was that participation would have the effect of increasing retail prices and those customers who did not use credit cards, *or who were prevented from doing so because they had been refused by credit card companies* (companies are very selective in choosing holders), would be compelled to subsidise the cost of the scheme and thus to contribute to the benefit accruing only to the bank and the credit card company, without gaining any advantage whatsoever for themselves. The National Chamber of Trade has adopted a similar attitude.

Criminal vulnerability of credit cards is great. Cards are easily stolen, "borrowed" from the purse or wallet of the holder, used fraudulently, and then returned without the holder being the wiser until he receives his monthly invoice (he has to pay a percentage service charge on the whole or a specified part of the amount for which credit is allowed). Cards are relatively easy to alter, forge, or duplicate, and immediate detection is still almost impossible if the work is from the hands of a technically competent criminal.

The size and shape of cards has resulted in accidental misuse, as when one was accidentally dropped, instead of a visiting card, into the letter-box of a house one dark evening by an American visitor who was trying to contact British friends for a few hours whilst waiting to change 'planes at London Airport. Not only did he discover too late that he had lost his "credit rating" and still had his visiting card, but he never saw his credit card again, having dropped it into the letter-box of a house not that of his friends! Having a smooth surface, cards easily fall out of wallets and pockets.

The convenience of the credit card scheme to businessmen and travellers results in the opportunity to make purchases without having to carry more cash than is necessary for minor needs, and the punched-hole or magnetic-ink encoding facilities provided on some cards are useful when industrial and other companies use this means in association with their employees' travelling and entertainments expense accounts. Like other methods of reducing the demand for cash, credit cards are admirable as long as their use does not raise retail prices and cause marketing restrictions, but, barring truly national coverage, there is only limited advantage in their use compared with, for example, travellers' cheques, which are internationally respected and encashable at many shops, hotels, railway stations, airports, etc., in all parts of the world. The National Federation of Sub-Postmasters some years ago came to an agreement whereby British sub-post offices dealt in American express cheques.

Before considering Giro Credit Transfer methods on a similar basis, it is essential that we should investigate the costs and convenience of the monetary transfer methods already considered.

2.3.   The Administrative Costs of Monetary Transfer

Bank-note, coin, cheque, postal- and money-order use is such a commonplace characteristic of everyday life in the United Kingdom that we tend to be oblivious to the cost of operating these systems. As a detailed breakdown of costs was given in *Giro Credit Transfer Systems* (p. 50–62), the reader will now be given only a few examples and hints on how to work out costs using his local conditions in office or home. Although every user —private as well as commercial— suffers the effects of these costs, the position in business is the more serious because of the cumulative effect and its influence on product and service prices. To be entirely competitive with our continental trading neighbours— especially in the EFTA and EEC groups—we ought to aim to establish a monetary transmission system as efficient and no more costly and complex than theirs.

In estimating the effect of monetary transfer costs the following operational and supply characteristics must be considered:

1. Office overheads. (Home overheads exist, too, contrary to the belief of some private individuals.)
2. The number of employees in the office comprising the basis of the assessment.
3. The cost of time taken in the performance of work connected with monetary transmission, for example:

   (a) Visits to the bank to pay in cheques, postal and money orders, etc.; the collection of cash for wages, etc.; the time spent in queuing at bank counters; the cost of special cash containers; the cost of transport by car or bus, etc.
   (b) The cost of time needed to store and retrieve payment records, and in collating documents and sequencing them.
   (c) The time required to duplicate written details as, for example, when more than one postal order has to be sent to make up a value, and the need to copy cheque

references, amounts, etc., before surrendering cheques with an accompanying lodgement form at a bank.

(d) The time needed to write out and check a dictated letter or advice note sent with a cheque, etc., and the addressing of an envelope. The time taken in the preparation of a receipt to confirm the arrival of a cheque (although there is no guarantee of its creditworthiness until after it has been processed by the bank) or the need to delay until it has been cleared and the taking up again of paperwork at this later stage.

(e) The time taken in recording details of cheques issued and the subsequent checking of safe arrival. The filing of counterfoils and cheque stubs, and their reconciliation with receipts or bank statements upon completion of the payment cycle.

(f) The time and cost allowance needed to search for and trace a payment lost in transit or as the result of fraud or theft.

4. Postage and stamp duty costs. Poundage.

5. The cost of stationery such as letter headings, carbon paper and carbon copies, invoice and receipt forms, envelopes, statement forms, and cheque forms printed to special order.

6. The cost of special security precautions required in the safeguarding of cash-handling and transit, and the protection from assault of all engaged in cash transactions and the storage or counting of cash. The safe-guarding of postal and money orders and the cost of time involved in making checks on stocks of them.

7. Loss insurance and personal injury insurance if separate from general insurance.

8. Bank charges, including purchase or rental of cash strong-boxes, safe deposits, etc.

A few of the above costs are involved in giro transactions, but it is advisable to make a comprehensive costing in order to obtain a clear impression of the amount associated with each method of monetary transmission. On the whole, giro methods encourage national standardisation extending beyond procedures to influence documentation and paperwork control, with the result that records are more uniform, easier to follow, and occupy less storage space. Of great importance is the fact that giro documentation is usually received pre-encoded and can be fed straight into an office computer-based accountancy, analysis, or recording mechanism.

2.3.1.   THE REMITTER'S ADMINISTRATIVE COSTS

These costs comprise:

1. The cost of obtaining a postal or money order from the Post Office including the time of the journey and queuing time, or the time of making a journey to and from a bank to pay in a cheque, etc. The cheque or stamp duty must be included.
2. The cost of time needed to retrieve office documentation relating to payments, the time taken to dictate, type, and check a letter or advice note to accompany the remittance, the addressing of an envelope and the filing away of duplicates of the communication.
3. The cost of letter postage and the postage of a receipt if the latter is required. (To provide a fair comparison with giro facilities, it is necessary to include the cost of preparing and sending a receipt.)
4. Office overheads and bank charges.

2.3.2.   THE BENEFICIARY'S ADMINISTRATIVE COSTS

These costs comprise:

1. The cost of sorting and routeing incoming post so as to extract letters containing remittances. The collation of these letters with the documents pertaining to the remittance enclosed. The checking of amounts and comparison with

issued statements or invoices retrieved from files, payment outstanding reminder boxes, etc.

2. The entry of cheque, postal or money order particulars in remittance received ledgers and the entry of remittances under the appropriate heading, i.e. "Cheque, Postal Order, Money Order" in the bank lodgement form with identifying references. Some firms insist that a record be made of cheque reference numbers and the issuing bank in addition to the remitter's name, address, the reason for payment, and amount. It is important to remember that unless the beneficiary does this, he has no record of the cheques (except for the value) after payment to his bank. The reverse applies to giro methods.

3. The cost of time to visit the bank and to return, including delays caused by queuing and verbal explanations when lodging cheques, postal orders, etc., must be included in time costed. If a beneficiary issues a receipt to the remitter before the latter's cheque has been cleared by the bank, this is done on trust and to try to clear the transaction quickly; if the beneficiary waits the 3 days usually needed to clear a cheque he has documents clogging his desk for at least that period. It is rather ironical that the cost of clearing a remittance is often greater for the beneficiary than for the remitter—who is spared bank documentation and a visit.

4. The cost of preparing a receipt, and stamp duty if the remittance was for £2 or more. The cost of stationery and postage.

5. Office overheads and bank charges.

2.3.3. CALCULATION OF COSTS

The examples have been simplified by assuming that losses do not occur in transit between the remitter and beneficiary, and that the latter sends the exact amount without prompting. The formulae give only an approximation but results show the folly of ignoring cost in monetary transmission methods. Although it is unlikely a firm would process only one remittance at a time, a unit remittance must be the basis of consideration to obtain a comparison of cost.

Note: All costs are expressed in pennies. All times are expressed in hours. Exceptions to these two general units are given.

1. *The office overhead cost per employee hour*

$$(C) = \frac{£a \times 240}{h \times e \times 52}$$

Where: a = the annual office bill in pounds sterling, for heating, lighting, cleaning, insurance, maintenance, rates, plant depreciation, services, rent, or lease.

h = employee's working week in hours.

e = number of employees.

2. *The employee's cost per working hour* $(S) = \dfrac{£s \times 240}{h \times 52}$

Where: s = the firm's liability for the employee's salary, pension, and insurance, in pounds sterling.

h = the employee's working week in hours.

3. *The cost of a particular operation* $(T) = \dfrac{t \times S}{60} + \dfrac{t \times C}{60}$

Where: t = time needed to perform operation.

= the sum of $t_1 + t_2 + t_3 + t_4$ and so on.

S = the employee's cost per working hour.

C = the office overheads cost per employee hour.

When: t_1 = time for journey to and from a bank or post office including counter queuing.

t_2 = time needed to dictate a letter or advice note to

accompany the remittance or a receipt, and checking it.

t_3 = time needed by a secretary–typist to prepare the
letter or advice note with file copy and envelope,
or to prepare a receipt and envelope.

t_4 = time needed for the remitter to effect reconciliation,
at an appropriate opportunity (usually when the
bank periodic statement arrives), of the payment
documents, the cheque or postal order stub or
counterfoil (respectively), and the receipt from the
beneficiary. Or the time needed for the beneficiary
to effect reconciliation (also usually when his
periodic statement arrives) between the lodgement
form record, and the remittance as recorded in his
books, and to dispatch a receipt accordingly. Compared with the immediate confirmation of creditworthiness and instantaneous disposal of related
documentation possible by giro methods, the
British conventional payment methods entail both
the remitter and beneficiary in the need to hold
papers in suspense until bank procedures have
been completed and therefore extend time needed
to process them to completion.

t_5 = time needed by the beneficiary to record details of
the cheque or postal order in his books (i.e.
if a cheque, the bank and serial number, etc.).
Also time taken in posting the receipt. It is necessary to make these allowances to obtain a true
comparison with giro methods.

4. *Ancillary costs* $(A) = m + n + p + r + u + v$

Where: m = cost of stationery (letter headings, envelopes,
receipt form, and printed compliment slip).

n = cost of postage.

p = cost of poundage.

r = cost of stamp duty.

u = cost of bank charges.

v = cost of transport by car or public vehicle to and from bank or post office.

5.   _The total cost to the remitter or beneficiary_ $(Y) = T + A$

   Note: For simplification in calculations, the following figures will be used in all examples. Bank charges vary with the customer's volume of business with his bank and their charging policy. Being unpredictable they are not included but should not be forgotten when comparing results; there are— in contrast—no charges for remittance transfers between giro account holders.

t_1 = 20 minutes.

t_2 = 4 minutes.

t_3 = 6 minutes.

t_4 = 8 minutes.

t_5 = 5 minutes.

m = 1.7d.

n = 4.0d. for a letter containing a cheque or postal order. 3.0d. for a receipt (by printed paper postage rate).

u = 0.0d. (bank charges not included, see above.)

v = car allowance is 7.5d. per mile and there is no parking meter charge.

The above values for time are reasonable only when an office has modern filing and record retrieval facilities and is laid out methodically; times should be doubled for many of the more haphazardly conducted offices, which seemingly comprise the majority at the time of writing this book.

The time taken by the remitter to complete a cheque or postal order form is about the same as for a giro form, and so is not included, i.e. this time period is a constant. Likewise, the time of taking the remittance letter to the postal dispatch box is a constant for all types of remittance method.

2.3.4. AN EXAMPLE OF MONETARY TRANSMISSION COST

In July 1966 the Directorate of Giro and Remittance Services published plans for the National Giro. Under the section entitled *The Transfer Service* on page 13 appeared the statement, "The minimum transfer will be 5s. 0d.", which implied that remittances for amounts less than this would have to be sent by bank cheque or credit transfer, or by postal or money order. Let us calculate the cost to a commercial remitter and beneficiary of transmitting 4s. 0d. by postal order. To make a fair comparison with giro methods it is necessary to ask the beneficiary to supply a receipt.

To simplify calculation we will assume that the office overheads of both the remitter and the beneficiary are the same, and that the employees of both firms are costing the same amount per annum. The reader will be able to vary these generalisations, if he wishes, using the equations already given.

1. *The office overhead cost per employee hour*

$$(C) = \frac{\pounds a \times 240}{h \times e \times 52}$$

Where: $\pounds a = \pounds 7500$ per annum.

$h = 42.5$ hours per week.

$e = 50$ employees.

$$= \frac{7500 \times 240}{42.5 \times 50 \times 52}$$

$$= 16.3d. \text{ per employee hour.}$$

2. *The employee's cost per working hour*

$$(S) = \frac{\pounds a \times 240}{h \times 52}$$

Where: £a = £1000 per annum.

   h = 42.5 hours per week.

$$= \frac{1000 \times 240}{42.5 \times 52}$$

$$= 108.6d. \text{ per}$$

$$\underline{\text{employee hour.}}$$

This is as far as we can take common cost characteristics for both the remitter and the beneficiary. We must now calculate the costs of each independently. We must find:

(a) The remitter's administrative costs of sending a postal order of value 4s. 0d.

(b) The beneficiary's administrative costs of banking and receipting the postal order.

For (a) the cost of the operation $T = \dfrac{t \times S}{60} + \dfrac{t \times C}{60}$

When: t = the sum of times:

   t_1 = visit to post office to purchase postal order: 20 minutes

   t_2 = dictation of letter or advice note and checking it: 4 minutes

   t_3 = typing the letter or advice note and preparing envelope: 6 minutes

   t_4 = reconciling documents, receipt, and counterfoil: 8 minutes

   Therefore t = 38 minutes

and $T = \dfrac{38 \times 108.6}{60} + \dfrac{38 \times 16.3}{60}$

   $= \underline{79.1d.}$

Ancillary costs $A = m + n + p + r + u + v.$

Where: m = cost of letter heading sheet and envelope = 1.7d.
n = cost of postage of letter to beneficiary = 4.0d.
p = cost of postal order poundage = 4.0d.
r = cost of stamp duty = 0.0d.
u = cost of bank charges nil = 0.0d.
v = cost of visiting post office to purchase postal order; 2 miles at $7\frac{1}{2}d$. per mile = 15.0d.

Therefore A = 24.7d.

Then the total cost to the remitter of $Y = T + A$
$$= 79.1 + 24.7$$
$$= 103.8d. \text{ or } 8s. \ 8d.$$

(b) The beneficiary's administrative costs of banking and receipting the postal order will be: $T = \dfrac{t \times S}{60} + \dfrac{t \times C}{60}$

When: t = the sum of times:

t_1 = journey to and from bank to deposit postal order: 20 minutes

t_2 = completing bank lodgement form and arranging a receipt: 4 minutes

t_3 = secretary–typist's preparation of a receipt and envelope: 6 minutes

t_4 = reconciliation of documentation, postal order amount, receipt, and bank periodic statement with lodgement form: 8 minutes

t_5 = copying of postal order details into payment record book, and posting receipt: 8 minutes

Therefore t = 46 minutes

and $\quad T = \dfrac{46 \times 108.6}{60} + \dfrac{46 \times 16.3}{60}$

$\qquad = \underline{95.7d.}$

Ancillary costs $A = m + n + p + r + u + v.$

Where: m = cost of receipt form and compliment slip if receipt not printed with firm's name and address, and envelope   =   1.7d.

n = cost of receipt postage   =   3.0d.

p = does not apply

r = cost of stamp duty on receipt is nil as the amount is less than £2   =   0.0d.

u = cost of bank charges not included for reasons given previously   =   0.0d.

v = cost of visiting bank to lodge postal order for payment; two miles at $7\frac{1}{2}d.$ per mile   =   15.0d.

Therefore $A = 19.7d.$

Then the total cost to the beneficiary of $Y = T + A$

$\qquad\qquad = 95.7 + 19.7$

$\qquad\qquad = \underline{115.4d.}$ or

$\qquad\qquad \underline{\text{approximately}}$

$\qquad\qquad \underline{9s.\ 7d.}$

So the cost to the remitter of transmitting 4s. 0d. by postal order is 8s. 8d., and to the beneficiary it is 9s. 7d. The value transmitted is not included.

Experience proves the need to emphasise that calculations based on a unit transaction are not unrealistic. Firstly, this is the only way to make comparisons and, secondly, both business and private individuals often must purchase, remit, and bank a single small denomination postal order. If the person values his time—and the techniques of efficiency *should* start at home like other good habits —he ought to be appalled by the waste of time and the complications of carrying out what ought to be a simple and entirely foolproof operation between himself and the beneficiary. As things are, he cannot escape from several basic charges beyond his power to alter. These costs are imposed by Government and comprise postal-order poundage and the postage of sending the remittance. Even if one ignores stationery and boot leather these costs remain and comprise an unreasonable percentage addition in proportion to the value of the postal order. For example:

Postal order value	Poundage	Postage stamp for letter	Imposed cost addition (%)
1s.	3d.	4d.	58
1s. 6d.	4d.	4d.	44
4s. 6d.	4d.	4d.	14

The Post Office provides no special service or security whilst holding the money in transition, as would be reasonable for making a poundage charge equalling 22 per cent of the value at 1s. 6d.

Like the iniquitous impediment to commercial efficiency—the stamp duty on cheques and receipts—the Government ought to have abolished the quaint old postal- and money-order system when Parliament legislated for a giro, and should have put in its place a single money-order system run on continental lines and entirely compatible with giro; but more of this later.

It is a blind hope that the cost of remittance and banking will decrease proportionately with the number of remittances handled. The non-standardisation of British invoices and statements and the great variety of payment methods multiplies paperwork immensely, and the absence of a giro-like facility has, in the past, made uniformity for computer processing uneconomical in the average general office. So an increase in the number of remittances over the basic unit considered in the above analysis will not necessarily reduce the unit cost per remittance and banking operation.

It should be emphasised again that the aim of the above example was to prove remittance costs cannot be shrugged off as being so minimal that they can be ignored in office administration. By the standards of continental giro countries, Britain's monetary transmission methods are unreasonably costly, complex, confusing, insecure, and productive of excessive paperwork.

2.4. Banking Costs and Competition

Until the establishment of the National Giro the commercial banks held a monopoly of business account banking. The threat of postal giro methods has started an immense upheaval in banking techniques and attitudes.

But even before Parliament legislated for a giro the banks were increasingly under fire from their public. The two main criticisms were:

1. The limited hours banks are open caused inconvenience.
2. The wide and almost unpredictable variety of methods by which banks calculated charges levied on customers' accounts for services rendered, and the general air of secrecy surrounding assessment processes, were unbusinesslike.

2.4.1.   BANKING HOURS AND A CHANGING SOCIAL STRUCTURE

An attitude of arrogance towards the public has been typical of many bankers and has not endeared them to either their customers or the public. It has been said bank officials are only human and tend to treat their customers according to the balance average of the customer's account and the officials' professional knowledge of the customer's resources. There are notable exceptions to this claim, but it has done much to colour the non-banking public's attitude to bankers as well as to make many small bank customers feel uncomfortable.

The charge of arrogance has been strengthened by the banks' retention of business hours, outmoded in a modern society; it is scarcely realistic to open at 10 a.m. and close at 3 p.m. on weekdays, or open at 9.30 a.m. on Saturdays and close 2 hours later.

These business hours are a survival from a leisurely age when bankers matched their business hours to the habits of a moneyed middle and upper class who regarded banking as a socially distinguishing symbol as much as a financial necessity. When the workers were off the streets in factory, office, and field, the manufacturer or landlord, squire or army officer, would drive into town for a discussion with friends and social equals as much as for business, and would be met with a show of deference by bank clerks selected for the social graces and "knowing their place".

Until the mid-1930's money in Britain was mostly in the hands of the upper and middle classes, and the majority of the public lived so near the bare sustenance line—many lived well below it —that every penny of income had to be put to good use, and the idea of bankers levying charges on all too slender balances was made even more repugnant by the need to forfeit valuable working hours to visit the bank.

But from the mid-1930's there started an almost imperceptible change in the distribution of money. The reasons were the rise of Hitler in Germany and, later, Mussolini's invasion of Abyssinia. The change was caused by the pressure placed on the British Government to order rearmament. Pressure initially was exerted by a series of furtive actions, such as a banner headline which appeared one morning, blatant and uncompromising, across the *Daily Express:*

BRITAIN NEEDS 2000 WAR PLANES

Under such heavy pressure from prophets of eventual war, the Government established a network of "shadow factories" charged with the task of pioneering weapons, establishing plans for the introduction of a massive armaments production programme if the international situation deteriorated, and the training of a core of experts in arms manufacture. Skilled and unskilled workers were increasingly in demand and monetary inducements were stepped up to encourage men and their families to move to new factories dispersed in what were hoped would be air-raid free areas if war came. Almost concurrently the trade unions' powers as negotiators of improved wages and working conditions increased, and the age-long deference expected of workers towards their masters started to be displaced by the demand that the wage should be equal to the task performed. The expanding demand for workers diminished fears that the demands for suitable monetary recognition would be met with sackings out-of-hand and unemployment on the dole.

With Britain's declaration of war on Germany in 1939, the demands of national security stretched manpower to the limit and, for the first time, the full-time employment of married women was accepted without question. The breakdown in social and class distinctions extended into the peace-time patterns of life from 1945 onwards and shaped the emerging welfare state. War-time rationing had established the principle of fair shares for all, and postwar reconstruction needs continued the gradual levelling of class distinctions of the pre-war variety. The possession of money and the ability to earn it—and to save some of what was earned—spread rapidly and without reference to accident of birth. The principle of full employment was in the making, in which there would, for many years to come, be more jobs than people to fill them, and trade unions would fight for ever better conditions of employment including a basic wage and the gradual elimination of exploitation with its pre-war fears of dismissal—often at less than an hour's notice—if a man complained he was being sweated. When a builders' labourer is likely to receive in wages in one month as much as a professional engineer's salary, he is not only likely to feel humiliated if his attempt to open a banking account is frustrated by his inability to use the bank's counter services in the same way as the professional engineer, but lunch-time on a building site is often too short and far-removed from banking branches to make a visit possible.

Even banking clerks are no longer content to be the deferential, self-effacing servants of customers which Victorian customs required them to be. The personal qualities of loyalty, initiative, integrity, intellect, etc., required of them are analogous to those of candidates for the civil service, which works a 5-day week and has many fringe attractions. Not unreasonably, bank clerks have campaigned for the removal of the nineteenth-century strictures on their freedom and for the same standard of working conditions enjoyed by most other professionals, and so the banks are faced with the dilemma that they may be obliged to offer a banking service only 5 days a week.

Although approximately 15 000 bank branches straddle Britain, the national coverage is poor because a branch of each of the "Big Five" is concentrated in towns of any size, with a resulting complete absence of bank facilities within miles of many country villages. As it is customary to site bank branches in or near the main business or shopping centres of a town the problem of access along traffic-congested streets involves more time for the factory worker than his lunch-break allows and, if he visits the bank on Saturday mornings, he is likely to spend some part of his one free shopping morning in queuing at the bank counter. In many English midland counties, as well as in many parts of Scotland, workers in local industry and agriculture would have to travel 7 miles or more to a bank branch in the local town, or to a village large and prosperous enough to support a bank branch. Local bus service fares are expensive additions to banking charges and in many rural areas the bus service is neither frequent nor fast enough to enable a worker to get to and from a bank in his lunch-break which, for agricultural workers, is often shortened in winter to make use of daylight, as well as being spent out in the fields far from the road to town.

It is obvious that commercial banks do not provide the national blanket coverage essential to a civilisation in which the possession of money is not only increasingly spread through all types of employment groups, but is also being earned increasingly at levels providing a margin above sustenance needs. The concentration of banks in certain localities and the exclusion of large areas and scattered groups from banking facilities; the restricted hours of business and the risk of unpredictable service charges, and the cumbersome and costly methods of operating the remittance service, all indicate the need for alternative facilities.

2.4.2. BANKING CHARGES

Coupled with the belief that banks live on "doing poor people out of their money" is the fear shared by many working people that bank charges are arranged by managers so as to discriminate against customers whose political or other affiliations, as disclosed by the cheques passed, conflict with the banks' vested interests, or with a particular bank manager's views. Many poorer people believe they would be helpless once they have opened a bank account because, if they were to find it too expensive to keep on, they would be faced with the alternative of closing it and sustaining heavy financial loss—in the form of a sort of financial forfeit of their balance to placate branch employees' tempers—or of staying with the bank and feeling helpless in what they imagine may be a slow but relentless process of being sucked dry of their savings, as charges mount.

But since about the mid-twentieth century not all the anxiety has been concentrated among the non-banking public. Some bankers have been fearful that the banks' expansionist aims may prove successful more rapidly than the handling equipment can grow to cope with demand. Although the 1961 programme of bank automation was speeded up to try and forestall further demands for a giro, there are not a few customers who nostalgically decry the elimination from statements of the former details of debits and credits in favour of coded abbreviations and the continuation of bank charges at former or greater levels despite the greater work thrown on the customer to keep a note of cheque serial numbers against cheques issued, etc.; some banks no longer issue cheque stubs adjacent to cheques and concurrently printed with details of each, so the customer has much more record-keeping to do. Another, and possibly far more serious effect of automation, is that a customer can seldom obtain at his bank an immediate statement of his account. Usually, a bank clerk has to telephone the bank's computer centre for this information, and during lunch-breaks or on Saturday mornings when counter staff are busy, the customer may be told his request is too embarrassing to receive immediate attention.

Since March 1961 Scottish banks have operated on a fixed-charge schedule with a minimum of 6*d.* for each debit entry, with an off-setting allowance on a minimum monthly credit balance of 6*d.* per £100 per month. This scale applies to private accounts only, and has given Scottish banks a reputation envied by many an English bank manager harassed by customers' complaints of unreasonably high account charges, a controversy which broke into the correspondence columns of the financial press with considerable fury from about 1963 onwards.

The reticence of English banks to supply information which would enable charging policies to be discussed openly and impartially has only served to exacerbate feelings. Too often potential customers have been put off by vague promises and no written confirmation. Whilst collecting data for inclusion in *Giro Credit Transfer Systems* I was refused particulars of the charging policies on some banks because I was not one of their account holders. This sort of reply suggests they first ensnare a man and instal him as a customer, and then present him with an ultimatum on account charges. An amusing article reflecting the growing resentment against bank attitudes appeared in the *Sunday Express* of 7 February 1965, under the title "Are You Happy With the Way Your Bank Treats You?" Written by Bernard Harris, the article was illustrated with the sketch reproduced in Fig. 21.

The report, *Bank Charges*, compiled by the Prices and Incomes Board (see Bibliography 2.1.5) suggests these are now cut pretty close to the bone of profitability. Banks still holding their customers to ransom will be the first to feel the chill wind of the National Giro's simple and cost-free credit transfer machinery. Even the banks' own credit transfer free service for customers and the 6*d.* per shot service for the public may not prove as attractive to the non-giroist as the 9*d.* per shot service offered 6 days per week (public holidays excluded) throughout normal shopping hours by

FIG. 21. The cartoonist of the *Sunday Express* saw the counter service difficulties of the banks in this light-hearted vein of humour in February 1965.

nearly all Britains' 23 000 sub-post offices and 2000 Crown post offices. Every community—however poor, remote, or small—is entitled to Post Office services. The same criteria does not apply to bank branch location.

The cost and time that would be needed to extend commercial banks to provide comparable national coverage to that of the Post Office is immense. Whilst the banks are currently engaged in modernising their existing structure to make it competitive with the National Giro—at a cost of over £100 million for computers and ancillary equipment—it is unlikely they will be able to attempt geographical expansion. They cannot increase customer charges without risk of losing customers. It seems likely they will increasingly adopt the business patterns of commercial banks in other European giro countries.

2.5.   The Post Office Savings Bank and Trustee Savings Banks

Trustee savings banks originated in the early nineteenth century with the object of encouraging communal thrift. Their conduct was regularised by Parliament in 1817.

By the mid-nineteenth century the growth of trustee savings banks lagged behind the nation's need for a general and vigorous savings movement; from 78 banks in 1817 the number had increased to just over 600 by the turn of the half-century, and 15 counties still had no facilities whatever.

The Post Office policy planners were mapping out a course for the expansion of its services so as to embrace activities in any way related to communications. The idea of a Post Office associated savings bank caught their imagination and, in 1861, the Post Office Savings Bank was established. Howard Robinson says, in his book *The British Post Office: A History*:

"In the latter years of the nineteenth century a number of other services, not strictly of postal character, were taken on by the Post Office. They were added because the numerous local post offices scattered over the land were convenient centres for various activities, and also because some of the services, such as those performed by the telegraph and telephone, seemed but extensions of postal communications. At any rate, they served to add enormously to the size of the growing department in the last quarter of the nineteenth century. It became more than ever the chief department of the government for serving the public.

But the architects of the POSB soon found that establishment of the new service was one thing and its expansion quite another. The commercial banks' fear of competition caused them to make strenuous efforts to contain the POSB within its original confines of activity. The interest earned by account holders was fixed at 2.5 per cent per annum—a rate which has not changed to this day despite the high interest rate trends of modern times. As a means of laming facilities further, for example, the POSB did not win the right to introduce the cheque-like warrant system until 1931.

Although impeded from introducing services which commercial bankers believed would make the POSB a challenge to their interests, the POSB was recognised abroad as a model for other countries to copy. By the time its first centenary was being observed in 1961 it had earned the distinction of being the "poor man's bank" and was the trusted depository for the money of millions of working people and children. But of as great interest was a development of the Austrian Post Office Savings Bank which, on 13 January 1883, was inaugurated by Emperor Frans Josef (1848–1916) on what *The Times* of the day called "the English model".

The first director of the Austrian POSB, Dr. Georg Coch, established a special facility based on the principles of the Venetian Banca Giro (see section 1.8.1), and, by modifying and modernising these ideas, provided nineteenth-century Austria with a financial institution which carried the country safely through an acute crisis and was found so valuable that it was retained. This facility—the Post Office giro—was eventually taken up and adapted to local conditions in other European countries and from them spread to Africa, Asia, and to islands in the Pacific Ocean. In 1961, of all Western European countries only Ireland, Greece, Portugal, Turkey, Spain, Iceland and the United Kingdom had not joined the giro 'club'.

But it is some consolation that the National Giro is a direct descendant of the Austrian Post Office Saving Bank's giro, and the Bank itself was copied from the British model of a POSB.

NOTE

At lectures given since the above was written I have been criticised for claiming that the Giro idea originated in Venice. It has been pointed out that the frontispiece picture caption of Dr. Georg Coch in *Giro Credit Transfer Systems* credits him with originating giro principles. As Dr. Coch was the originator of the Post Office Giro and *Giro Credit Transfer Systems* was entirely devoted to describing the development and merits of this particular application of giro principles, the caption is accurate.

But to those who still insist that Dr. Coch was the father of giro banking, I can offer no better advice than to consult a book published in Venice in 1847, when Coch was 5 years old; a copy is in the library of the Italian Institute of Culture, London. The title is *Venozia e Le Sue Lagune*, and reference to Banca Giro is in volume 1, part 1, pp. 364–7. The diplomat and military administrator, Jacopo Foscarini, who died in 1602, is named as the instigator of Banca Giro.

The writings of other authorities suggest that Giro principles had been discussed from about the twelfth century. Also, some claim the Banca della Piazza di Rialto was known informally as Banca Giro from its foundation, put by some writers at 1584, and by others at 1587.

CHAPTER 3

Giro Banking Organisation

3.1. Legislative Danger

There are already some indications of public disquiet at what appears to have been the secret way in which giro legislation was rushed through Parliament. More than one person who, in the past, has taken an active part in campaigning for or opposing government proposals has complained he knew nothing of giro until long after the Directorate of Giro and Remittance Services had issued plans. The same sort of person usually observes that whilst agreeing in principle with the reform, he very strongly resents the way in which it was brought into being. In particular, he charges the Government with secretly legislating without the electorate's knowledge or consent for a measure that will intimately affect the life of everybody in Britain.

Of all great postwar reforms stimulated by parliamentary legislation, the giro has benefited least from the public praise or condemnation, salutation or satire, suggestions or counter-proposals which customarily assail attempts to modernise national institutions for the greater advantage of the community.

It is true the giro campaign and legislative measures did not follow exactly the same path as some other great reforms of the postwar years. The pressure of events and circumstances made widespread public support at all levels impossible to organise, but it was never far from the minds of those involved in pressing this reform through that the argument in its favour was weakened by the very fact that giro had never been thrown into the forum of public examination and discussion.

The pressure of events was obvious to experts in banking, economics, and export marketing, but it was not easy to convince quickly the average trade unionist, politically active worker, or housewife that a great reform in banking method was both urgent and essential. Britain's involvement with the Scandinavian group of European Free Trade Association countries in particular made it abundantly clear that until the cumbersome and costly British monetary remittance system was modernised to provide equal facilities to those for so long used in Sweden and Denmark, Norway and Switzerland, Austria, and practically every other major continental country, it would not only be stupid to consider any other close association—such as membership of the European Economic Community—but that British business administration would continue to be loaded with a mass of irritating and unproductive paperwork processes which have little effect other than to raise production costs and central administration inefficiency.

Giro campaigning and legislation has been compared with the postwar nation-wide movement in support of the free medical service under the National Health Insurance Act, and it has been asked why a similarly strong body in support of giro did not emerge, particularly as the workers had no great fondness for the commercial banking system. Those of us who campaigned for a giro often wished we could stir public support on a similar scale, but there were two main reasons why this seemed impossible at the time. The reasons were:

1. The inherent British mistrust of foreign ideas and institutions.
2. The absence of an English language vocabulary for giro.

We would have liked everybody to have an opinion on giro and its possibilities, just as most people had an opinion on the morality of nominating the state as the guardian of the nation's health to the extent of providing free medicine for the sick and old. But the main difference between giro legislation and health legislation was that everybody held a personal view—based on experience—of the legislative needs for health planning. Practically nobody had any experience of giro operation, and very few even knew the meaning of the word; it did not appear in any but the most expensive dictionaries and in no encyclopedias.

So what should one have done when external events as much as internal national trends were pressurising the monetary remittance services' inefficiency, and inability to cope with the demands of a rapidly developing computer-centred civilisation? Should one have delayed legislation until every member of the electorate had learned to trust the foreign-originated giro idea and had developed a vocabulary of English expressions to discuss it, or should one have adhered to the course that eventually was followed? If legislation had been delayed the probability is that British commerce would have been brought to a standstill by 1970.

Parliamentary legislation for giro is a classical example of a comparatively small number of people having to act in a prophylactic capacity to ward off the ultimate effects of a steadily deteriorating condition in national organisation. But the point is taken that there is inherent danger when Parliament legislates for a reform as great in administrative reorganisation magnitude as giro, and the people on whose lives it will increasingly impact feel they have been neglected at the campaign stage.

Now let us consider why it was so difficult to include more people in the campaign.

3.2.   The Terminology of Foreign Systems

Giro methods form a constituent part of everyday life for most of our European neighbours, and in daily talk they refer to the various forms and methods as much as bank cheques and credit transfer, postal and money orders are mentioned by people in Britain.

Modern giro methods originated in the German-language part of Europe and, although so many countries have adopted the system, its absence in an English-speaking country posed problems of terminology when the campaign for its establishment in Britain was started about 1946.

Never quick to agree that some foreign methods and things might be better than native products, the British have, in general, been loath to examine the claims made for this type of banking, and were much put off or confused by the name. One group who asked for a lecture about giro, for example, was disappointed when they found it is not connected with a navigational system for satellites. The absence of a central source of information on the subject, its neglect by dictionary publishers, and its almost total exclusion from the pages of national newspapers and magazines as well as from the programmes of the sound and television broad-casting authorities, on the grounds that the public would not be interested—an attitude expressed as recently as 1967 by the BBC, by the way—served to stop the public from finding out about giro. Undoubtedly, pressure from the vested interests of banking had a good deal to do with boycotting publication of information about a possible alternative to the banks' remittance services, although the effect would also tend to block British computer development and sales. When lecturing to a rotary club about giro I was once told by bankers that I was more dangerous to them than the entire British Communist Party.

In the campaign for a giro the first essential was to produce a vocabulary of English expressions that would encourage dis-cussion. This was not easy, as I found when I wrote the first English language pamphlet on the subject, *Giro: Europe's Wonder Bank*, published in 1952. Perhaps fortunately, the pamphlet had a circulation of only about 1000 copies, because I soon afterwards found the vocabularly I devised was not entirely satisfactory. To improve it for *Giro Credit Transfer Systems*, I tried to relate terminology to a more functional approach.

Even still, the expression *giro* is causing confusion. For example, I have been told it should be written *G.I.R.O.*—because a Labour Party official leaflet writes it like this—and the letters stand for "George's International Remittance Organisation". It is entirely true that the Labour Party's headquarters did distribute thou-sands of leaflets making reference to giro in this way, and the rumour seems to have developed that the letters stand for a reform negotiated by George Brown, M.P., when he was the Minister of Economic Affairs.

A primary essential for intelligent discussion of any topic is general agreement on the meaning of words, so let us lay down an English-language vocabulary our continental giro friends will also recognise.

3.2.1. THE DEFINITION OF *GIRO*

Giro is derived from the Greek γυρος, pronounced *guros* and meaning "ring", "circle", or "circuit". It is pronounced *geero*, with a long *ee* as in *jeer;* the *g* may be like that in *go*, or like the *j* in *jeer*. To avoid confusion with a gyroscope, or gyro for short, it is preferable to say *geero* or *jeero*.

A giro is a comprehensive system of monetary and credit transfer services offering the simpler parts of banking and arranged with respect to a clearing centre organised as a common inter-mediary for the processing of transactions between the remitter and beneficiary. The system's basic requirements are that services shall be worked with the minimum cost and operational time consistent with communication essentials, and that both parties to a transaction shall receive an immediate confirmation with details of it; also that documentation shall be minimal consistent with information exchange needs. By nature a giro is now heavily dependent on computer-centred automatic machinery for the secure and accurate handling of the massive turnover of public and account holders' debitings and creditings; and to provide essentials such as rapid print-out of account statements, business integration capability maximisation, and the fullest joint advantages to the nation and account holders. The latter usually receive services free except for transactions with external organisations and people.

The system imposes rigid adherence to a particular sequence of operations and the use of officially approved stationery and forms, and users must observe the few regulations essential for the trouble-free working of the various processes. Although not necessarily associated with a Post Office structure, a giro achieves its highest degree of efficiency when integrated with services peculiar to Post Office internal organisation, and without exception has taken root primarily within the Post Office framework of every country adopting the system. Broad principles of organisation are regulated by the Universal Postal Union, at Berne, Switzerland.

3.2.2.   THE THREE BASIC SERVICES

The three basic services require the use of forms specially designed and standardised for the various computer-encoding operations they will eventually actuate. They are:

1. The *inpayment form*. This is used by a person without a giro account to transfer money to a giro account holder.
2. The *transfer/deposit* form. This is used when a giro account holder orders a credit transfer from his account to another giro account holder.
3. The *payment order* form. This is used when a giro account holder wishes to arrange a payment in cash to a person with no giro account.

The *transfer/deposit* form is also used when the giroist pays cash to his account, at a Post Office.

3.2.3.   OTHER EXPRESSIONS

Brevity of expression and clarity of meaning are important features in the successful operation of a giro.

To avoid using the mouthful, *giro account holder*, I coined the expression *giroist*. A *person without a giro account* is a *non-giroist*. These expressions have passed into public use.

For the same reason it is preferable to use *inpayment* instead of *credit*, and *remitter* instead of *payer* or *debtor*. *Outpayment* is preferable to *debit*, and *beneficiary* is preferable to *payee*, *creditor*, or *recipient*. There are fine shades of difference between these terms, but *inpayment* and *outpayment* are immediately self-explanatory of the way money is going with respect to an account, and *remitter* and *beneficiary* indicate at once which is the loser and which the gainer.

The National Giro will provide ancillary services such as a means of transferring credit from a giroist's account to his own, or another's, joint stock bank account. This service will involve use of a *Giro/JSB credit transfer* form.

Compared with most other European giros the National Giro is opening with a bare bones service. As the number of giroists increases above the minimum required to make the service profitable, the range of services will increase and giro terminology will grow.

It is appropriate to note the various continental names by which giro is known:

1. In Danish:	*Postkonto* or *girokonto*
2. In Dutch:	*Postcheque- en Girodienst*
3. In Finnish:	*Postisiirtotilit*
4. In French:	*Compte courant postal* or *C.C.P.* or *Chèques postaux* or *Chèque et virements postal*
5. In German:	*Postscheckkonto* or *Postcheck*
6. In Italian:	*Conti corriente postal* or *Chèques postali*
7. In Norwegian:	*Postgirokonto*
8. In Swedish:	*Postgiro*

The world's giro countries are shown in Fig. 22. Britain is practically the only one to omit *post* or *postal* from the name of its service—a useful reminder to the public of the administrative headquarters. Although *Postgiro* is a registered business name privately owned in Britain, an offer was made to transfer ownership to the General Post Office when they were planning the Giro. The offer was refused. Foreign experience suggests *Post Giro* would have been more attractive than *National Giro*. The former expression rolls comfortably off the tongue and is understood

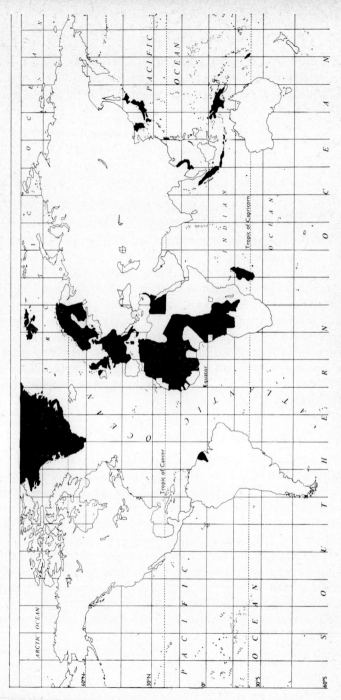

Fig. 22. The world of giro countries is marked in black.

universally. As the commercial banks have a Bank Giro, it will be essential for advertisements, etc., to carry *National* as a means of distinguishing which giro is meant. Which do you prefer? Which makes most impact?

Pay to	*Pay to*	*Pay to*
POST	BANK	NATIONAL
GIRO	GIRO	GIRO
4278	4278	4278

3.2.4.   THE GIRO AUTHORITY

The British authority is the Directorate of Giro and Remittance Services, a department of the General Post Office, based on the Giro Clearing Centre, Orrell Lane, Bootle, Lancashire. This coastal town at the mouth of the River Mersey, 5 miles north of Liverpool on the A5036 road, was chosen for its geographically central position with relation to air, sea, and land traffic to all parts of the United Kingdom. There was also an urgent need to diversify local employment opportunities. The architects' model of the Giro building, placed on a 15-acre site, is shown in Fig. 23. The National Giro is a scheduled component of the Post Office Corporation.

3.3.   Features Peculiar to a Post Office Giro

The process of opening a business or private account differs little from that of the joint stock banks. Practically everyone over 16 years of age is eligible and only has to fill up an application form and hand it, with a minimum deposit of £5, to a Post Office clerk. Alternatively, the application may be sent to the Directorate of Giro and Remittance Services.

In return, the applicant is issued with a number comprising 7 digits for a business account or 9 digits for a private one. Special envelopes and forms are supplied at cost price and a levy is made to cover stamp duty on forms subject to this tax.

All forms are pre-printed with the account holder's name,

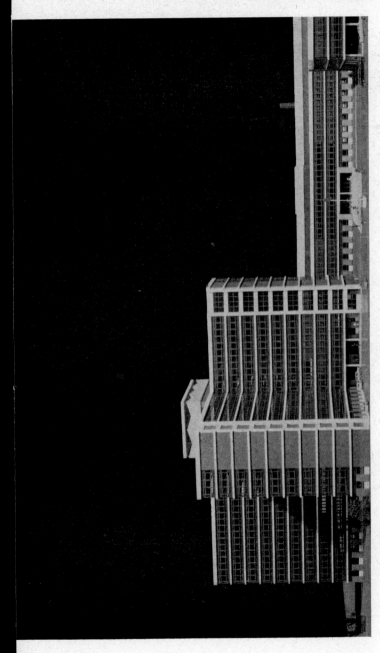

Fig. 23. The National Giro Centre at Bootle, Lancashire, designed by the Ministry of Public Buildings and Works and shown as an architects' model.

address, and account number. The envelopes are pre-printed with the address of the Giro Clearing Centre and franked postage free. All transactions between the account holder and the Centre must be negotiated using only these forms and envelopes.

3.3.1.   FEATURES PECULIAR TO GIRO ACCOUNT WORKING

The main features making a Giro different are:

1. No interest is paid on balances at the Giro Centre.
2. No overdrafts are allowed.
3. No loans are given.
4. Unlawful use of an account is liable to lead to its closure, without notice, by the Postmaster-General.
5. State security is guaranteed.
6. The single National Giro Centre is responsible for performing all the crediting and debiting operations ordered by non-giroists to giroists, between giroists, and from giroists to non-giroists. In this immense task the Centre operates as a single integrated unit located at one site, and so has the effect of drastically limiting the mass of inter-banking transactions customarily needed to process monetary transfers through the joint stock banks' clearings.
7. All forms used by the public and by giroists are provided with a space sufficient in size to accommodate a message or order up to about 60 words maximum length, for the beneficiary's attention; although this facility spares the remitter from having to write a separate letter or advice note, no charge is made. The section of the form bearing the message, etc., also details the amount sent, the date, the name and address of the remitter, and—if a giroist—his account number. The Giro Clearing Centre eventually passes on this section, or confirmation note, to the beneficiary to give him full details of the payment.
8. A giroist is entitled to receive from the Giro Clearing Centre a statement of account the day following that on which a change has been made in the balance of his account. The

statement will be accompanied by the confirmation note(s) described in 7 and/or by debit confirmation note(s) comprising section(s) from any *transfer/deposit* or *payment order* forms he has sent to the Centre for clearance.

9. The system is planned to give the public the utmost encouragement to adopt credit transfers in preference to all other types of monetary transaction and, by sending postal instructions instead of making visits to banks and post offices, to reduce the demand for counter services.

10. The system is also planned to work on a minimum information transfer basis. The three pieces of information needed to negotiate a transfer are only the remitter's and the beneficiary's account numbers, and the amount in the form of a number. This simplification in payment procedure is a psychologically sound way of persuading people to pay.

11. Giro *inpayment* forms can be incorporated in advertising material to create a high-impact sales aid. Pre-giro Britain had no counterpart service.

12. A giroist can make a demand withdrawal up to £20 at his local post office, or up to £50 maximum at any post office after clearance by the Giro Clearing Centre.

13. All but a few of the smallest post offices will handle giro business. This provides the public with national banking coverage 6 days a week (public holidays excepted), throughout working hours.

14. Giro directories containing account holders' names, addresses, and numbers will be on sale, and at post offices for reference.

3.4. The Basic Pattern

All transactions are converted to a simple basic pattern comprising the transfer of money as credit from an account holder *A*, through the Giro Clearing Centre's debiting and crediting machinery, to an account holder *B*.

In effect, this means the deduction of an amount X from account number A, and the addition of amount X to account number B.

This is a very easy operation for a computer to perform provided the instructions are presented in a code compatible with the computer's command mechanism. It is also necessary that the results printed out by the computer should be got away quickly to account holders A and B. This latter requirement may seem irrelevant but is essential if the risk of an overdraft as the result of some following transfer is to be avoided. An instruction resulting in an overdraft would block the computer with respect to the account concerned.

When either the remitter or the beneficiary are not personally account holders they obtain access to the system through a post office which, in effect, stands proxy for them.

The three basic services provide facilities for the transmission of remittances and confirmation of receipt between:

1. Non-giroists and giroists.
2. Giroists.
3. Giroists and non-giroists.

When the cost to the Giro authority is lessened or, in terms of the convenience gained, not appreciably increased per unit transaction, ancillary services are grafted on and worked in association with any of the three basics. In Britain the ancillaries comprise:

1. Automatic debit transfer.
2. Collection under a standing order.
3. Periodic payment collection.
4. Issue of traveller's cheques and foreign currency.
5. An international transfer service.

3.5. Basic and Other Services

The flow diagrams are part of the series used earlier to illustrate bank and Post Office monetary transmission methods and, like them, depict instalment payment procedures between a customer and a hire purchase finance house, but also are true for any type of payment by the method shown, by anybody.

The systems outlined are based on the best characteristics of continental giros and do not relate entirely to the National Giro pattern. All but three continental postal giros have no limit on the amount transferred and consequently commercial giroists automate their entire monetary transfer with one set of machine-read forms and tapes. The National Giro's bar on amounts below 5s. makes this impossible for British giroists unless they use the Bank Giro. To provide the maximum economy in computer equipment for British giroists it is essential that Bank and National Giro documents, forms and magnetic tapes should be standardised so that only one type of machine encoding or reading unit is needed. National Giro forms are encoded with optical character recognition letters and figures type "B" of the European Computer Manufacturers' Association.

The advantages and success of giro depends tremendously on account holders making their account numbers known. *The Giro Directory* is like a large telephone directory and gives account holders on a cross-reference, by name or number. It can be seen in all post offices and public libraries or purchased at a nominal price.

But keen giroists print their account number on notepaper, trade and visiting cards, invoices and statements, advertisements, catalogues, etc., and even emboss it on perishable articles to expedite reordering.

How much easier it is to ask a potential customer to pay to:

GIRO 0145 709

than to require him to write down or remember to pay to:

David Adams,
South Street,
Corstorphine,
Midlothian.

Even if a PO box number address is used with the name of the person or firm, it is far longer than a simple number of a giro account.

3.5.1. How the Public Sends Money to a Giroist

Figure 24 shows the sequence of operations, paperwork, and costs of a remittance. In this instance the customer or remitter has received from the finance house a giro *inpayment form*, and Fig. 25 illustrates a typical example issued by a Swedish housing or building society to one of its tenants. The finance house or building society has used its own computer to pre-encode the customer's mortgage instalment amount and ledger reference, in

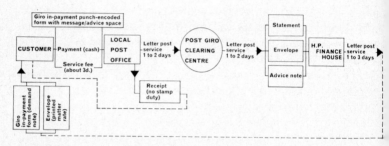

Fig. 24. This flow diagram traces out the main operations when a non-giroist member of the public makes a remittance to a giroist. At the time this diagram was drawn the service fee for this category of remittances, or vice versa, was 3*d*. The National Giro fee for the same type of service is 9*d*.

both typewritten and punched-hole characters, but has left the customer to write his own name and address.

Alternatively, a customer who does not receive a form from the finance house can obtain a free *inpayment* form blank at the Post Office and completes it by writing his name and address, the amount of money he is remitting, the date, and the name, address, and account number of the giroist finance house. If he knows his ledger reference, he writes it in the message space, or may have some other message, or a query, to send.

An *inpayment* form may come into the possession of people in other ways too. It may be found as an advertisement insert in a magazine like that in Fig. 26, which was part of a sales promotion campaign mounted by a Swedish organisation; or it may form part of an advertisement in a magazine or catalogue.

Irrespective of the way the *inpayment* form was acquired the non-giroist remitter makes payment by taking the completed form, the remittance, and the service fee (9*d.* in Britain) to a Post

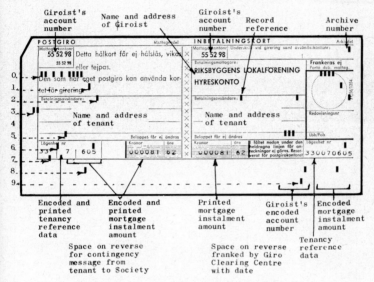

Fig. 25. This typical pre-encoded giro inpayment form was issued by a Swedish building society to one of its tenants to encourage payment by the means outlined in Fig. 24. The numbers 0–9 placed against the left side of the form enable the reader to trace out the location of punched holes corresponding to numbers. The British National Giro form encoding will use printed or typewritten figures capable of being read by electronically operated sensors, which will transmit the information in a form acceptable to the computers.

Office, and hands the three items to a clerk, who issues a receipt confirming the remitter has completed his part of the transaction; and the responsibility now rests with the Post Office.

At the end of each day's work, the Post Office clerk packs all the giro *inpayment* forms received into a distinctively coloured and standard-sized envelope together with two copies

LIDINGÖ GILLE
LIDINGÖ
—

ÅRSKORT

i

LIDINGÖ GILLE

för innevarande år.

Årsavgiften betald med fem (5) kronor, kvitteras genom postverkets kvitto
på beloppet.

Stockholm, poststämpelns datum.   *Skattmästaren*

Här kan avsändaren fästa postens kvitto.

Postgirokonto nr 3 72 60

Inbetalning sker på postanstalt med användande av vidfogade inbetalningskort. Innehavare av postgirokonto bör dock lämpligen begagna sig av girering, varvid någon portoavgift icke utgår.

Före inbetalning på postanstalt skall detta meddelande avskiljas av Eder och behållas.

POSTGIRO   **INBETALNINGSKORT**   Arkivdel

Kupong (mottagardel)	Avsändarens namn och adress	Plats för frankering
Postgirokonto nr **3 72 60**		Ifylles med bläck eller maskin
Belopp **5** kr — öre	Belopp **5** kr — öre	
Avsändarens namn och adress	Betalningsmottagare (namn och adresspostanstalt) *Lidingö Gille* *Lidingö*	Postgirokonto nr **3 72 60**
Meddelande till betalningsmottagaren	Lbb/pob kvitto nr	Redovisningsnr	Redov. postanstalt
	Bl 703 ET (Nov 61) * Pv tr Sth	

FIG. 26. This is a Swedish example of the use of a giro inpayment form in
association with an advertisement. This is a potent type of market promotion
of which Britain had no equivalent in pre-giro days.

of a record sheet detailing all payments and the total received; the two sheets and his third copy carry the branch Post Office address, date, and giro account number. The envelope is sealed and sent by overnight post to the Giro Clearing Centre where the size and colour of the envelope automatically routes it to the *inpayment* form encoding and checking section. All the forms are checked visually and encoded with the originating Post Office's account number, the amount remitted, and the beneficiary's account number. The individual remittance amounts are totalled and compared with the record sheets sent by the branch Post Office; one sheet is kept for Centre records and the other is receipted and dispatched to the remitting Post Office branch as confirmation.

Each *inpayment* form is microfilmed for Centre records, and then fed into the computer's automatic debiting and crediting mechanism.

It will be seen that the forms in Figs. 25 and 26, are made of two sections divided by a vertical line of X's. The section—or confirmation note—at the left is the beneficiary's credit confirmation note and has the message space on its reverse side. The section on the right is the remitter's debit confirmation note, and is retained at the Giro Centre's stores until there is no further question of queries regarding the payment being raised by either the non-giroist remitter or the originating branch post office.

In its journey through the computer's mechanism the encoding on the form actuates, in association with stored information concerning the account balances held by the remitter and beneficiary respectively, the statement print-out machinery and the form section separation machinery. The two sections—or confirmation notes—are separated and each is married to its associated statement of account; one for the remitter and the other for the beneficiary. As the account holder's name and address are also printed out automatically on the statement sheet it is only necessary for an automatic machine to pick up the statement and credit confirmation note addressed to the beneficiary and insert them in a window envelope (through which the address on the statement is clearly seen), to seal the envelope, and route it to the mail outlet dealing with postal dispatches to the addressee's area. A similar operation is undertaken with respect to the statement for the remitting post office branch.

This is a simplified description to indicate the various steps which, indeed, may seem mysterious to the non-technical observer when he hears of the huge number of transactions a Giro Clearing Centre has to perform in a single day; the number of *inpayment* forms alone may run into several millions. To prevent risk of discrepancies, the originating Post Office's statement sheets will be presented in a single continuous read-out and compared with the total amount shown on the record sheet sent with the *inpayment* forms and the total will then be deducted from the branch Post Office's credit balance at the Giro Centre.

The time period from when the transfer instructions are received from the originating branch Post Office until the Giro Clearing Centre dispatches the respective statements to the remitter and beneficiary, is unlikely to be more than 24 hours. As giro service envelopes are so distinctive and easy to recognise in postal sorting offices, the complete cycle of operations involved in negotiating a credit transfer and receiving confirmation of its success is unlikely to exceed 48 hours except at weekends and on public holidays.

The Swedish giro statement, credit confirmation note, and window envelope shown in Fig. 27 are typical of the communication giroists receive. The statement details:

1. The name and address of the giroist beneficiary.
2. His account number.
3. The postal sorting code.
4. The date of the Centre transaction.
5. (Upper). The account balance at the opening of business. (Lower). The account balance at the close of business.
6. The credit additions (in black ink) and the debits (in red ink) during the day in which a change occurred.

Note: The credit confirmation note shown is part of a giroist's *transfer/deposit* form (the remitter's account number appears

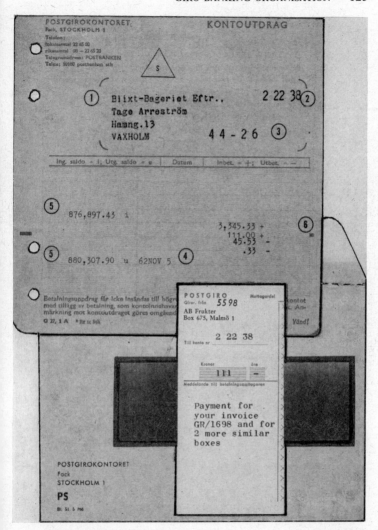

FIG. 27. This illustrates the window envelope containing the statement (top), and credit confirmation note or slip, which the Swedish giroist beneficiary receives the day following that in which a change has been made in the balance of his account.

in print at the top of the note: 55 98, and the message space starts on this side). In all other respects this note is similar to that of an *inpayment* form, as will be seen by reference to Fig. 26.

Big account holders may find a magnetically encoded tape a more convenient way of receiving details of debits and credits than a written statement with accompanying confirmation notes —although these may be useful for visual checks and, being encoded, can be used to actuate sales analysis, market forecasting, and other equipment ancillary to the main computerised accountancy system of a finance house, building or housing society, etc.

It will be seen from the flow diagram in Fig. 24 how few the handling operations are and that, because the process of remittance progress is checked at every stage as well as being packed into a tight and routine time schedule, there is not only little opportunity for loss and error to creep in, but, if it does, it will be quickly spotted and remedied. Furthermore, the remitter and beneficiary have nothing to do except confirm the statements sent to them—by reference back to the balance on the immediately preceding statement—when they receive confirmation of the completion of the transfer operation; each party to the transaction is left with a permanent record in the shape of the confirmation note.

3.5.2.   HOW GIROISTS MAKE PAYMENTS TO EACH OTHER

Figure 28 outlines the sequence of operations, paperwork, etc., involved when a giroist remits to another giroist.

The *transfer/deposit* form shown in Fig. 29 was printed by the Dutch Giro Authority for one of its British account holders, but is typical of the type of form used in many European giro countries. The Giro Authority provides forms pre-printed with:

1. The giroist's account number (shown in this example as *145709*).

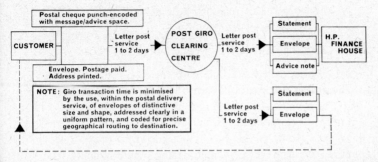

FIG. 28. This flow diagram traces out the sequence of operations when one giroist orders a remittance credit transfer to another giroist.

2. The giroist's name and address (shown in this example as:

> *Bookpostgiro*
> *Church Road*
> *FORD, Engeland*).

3. The chronological number of the form (5 in this example). This gives the original position of the particular *transfer/deposit* form in the book (like a cheque book).

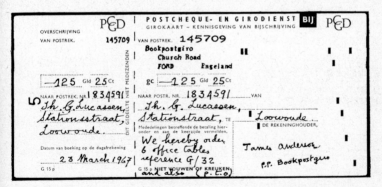

FIG. 29. This Dutch transfer/deposit form is typical of the postal cheques used by continental Europe's giroists in countries with computer-controlled giro centres.

The form is also punched-hole encoded to indicate:

(a) The chronological number 5, and a sorting code 6.
(b) The giroist's account number *145709*.

All number sequences start with the reference-level figure 0.

The giroist remitter completes the form by writing in the beneficiary's name, address, and account number, the amount of the remittance, and the date. He has the option of adding a message, order, etc. (some people have been known to draw dimensioned pictures of furniture they are ordering with payment). The form is authorised by the remitter's signature and is inserted in one of the postage-free envelopes pre-addressed to the Giro Clearing Centre, sealed, and dropped into a convenient letter-box to start its postal journey to the Giro Clearing Centre. On arrival, the content of the envelope is recognised by its shape and colour and it is rapidly and automatically routed to the section concerned with checking and encoding *transfer/deposit* forms. The remitter's written particulars are checked and his signature verified. The form is encoded in machine-readable characters with the remittance in figures and the beneficiary's account number.

The form is microfilmed for Centre records and starts its journey through the computer's debiting and crediting mechanism, following approximately the same set of operations as the *inpayment* form except that a statement is printed out for dispatch to both the remitter and beneficiary, and the respective confirmation note for each is sent with the accompanying statement. But, of course, either or both giroists may prefer to have their statement presented as a magnetically encoded tape if their respective accounts attract many debiting and crediting operations each day.

The Dutch *transfer/deposit* form shown in Fig. 29 has the remitter's debit confirmation note on the left of the broken vertical line, and the beneficiary's credit confirmation note at the right.

The flow diagram in Fig. 28 omits nothing and shows how very scientific and efficient basic giro is when worked between giroists.

3.5.3. How Giroists Make Payments to Non-giroists

The giroist remitter uses a *payment order* form similar to a *transfer/deposit* form except that the name of the non-giroist beneficiary is substituted for the giroist beneficiary's number.

The remitter completes the form by writing the beneficiary's name, address, nearest Post Office, the amount of the remittance, and the date; he authorises the form by signing it, and it is then sealed in one of the postage-paid pre-addressed envelopes, and dispatched to the Giro Clearing Centre.

The Centre's checking and encoding section carries out approximately the same routine as for a *transfer/deposit* form, except that the giro account number of the nominated Post Office is encoded as the beneficiary's account number and the form is embossed with a die-stamping machine to authorise it as a cash-on-demand voucher. The form then follows the same course through the debiting and crediting mechanisms of the computer as the *transfer/deposit* form, except that the credit is paid to the account of the nominated Post Office. The beneficiary's credit confirmation note—now the voucher—is posted to the non-giroist. On receiving it, he presents it for encashment at the nominated Post Office. To avoid risk of misappropriation he has to establish his identity. Some post giro authorities supply, for a fee of about 1*s.*, a special identity card bearing the holder's photograph. Payments made by a giroist to a non-giroist involve the former in a service charge which is debited to the account of the former; in Britain the charge is 9*d.* per transaction.

3.6. Bank Cheque and Giro Transfer/Deposit Remittance Methods Compared

Figure 30 illustrates a typical mail-inwards and accounts department documents flow sequence of a hire purchase finance house, building society, insurance company, direct mail order firm, electricity or gas supply undertaking, municipal rates department, etc., in pre-giro Britain.

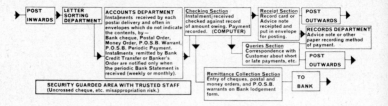

Fig. 30. This flow diagram illustrates the sequence of operations in a typical mail-inwards and accountancy department of a firm; in this instance the hire purchase instalments receiving section of a finance house.

Figure 31 illustrates the economies likely to be effected as a result of introducing giro methods. Mention is not made, however, of the likelihood of customers becoming more punctual in making payments as a direct result of simplification of payment processes and as a result of a reduction in methods cost.

There follows a comparison of the cost of the two methods, using the same figures, and making the same assumptions as were used in sections 2.3.3 and 2.3.4.

In section 2.3.4 the following were calculated:

1. *The office overhead cost per employee hour* $(C) = 16.3d.$

2. *The employee's cost per working hour* $(S) = 108.6d.$

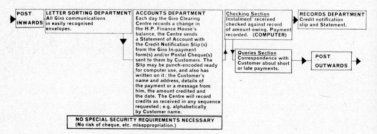

Fig. 31. This illustrates the same as Fig. 30, but after the establishment of a giro and its use for instalment collection.

3. *The cost of a particular operation* $(T) = \dfrac{t \times S}{60} + \dfrac{t \times C}{60}$

When: t = time needed to perform operation
    = the sum of $t_1 + t_2 + t_3 + t_4$ and so on,
and: t_1, etc., has the same value in minutes as given previously.

4. *Ancillary costs* $(A) = m + n + p + r + u + v$
Where: m, n, and so on have the same values as given previously.

5. *The total cost to the remitter or beneficiary* $(Y) = T + A$
    The cost of transmitting £3. 10s. 0d. by bank cheque will be
for
    (a) the remitter, (b) the beneficiary, as follows:

(a) *The cost to the remitter of transmitting* £3. 10s. 0d. *by bank cheque.*

3. $T = \dfrac{18 \times 108.6}{60} + \dfrac{18 \times 16.3}{60}$

    = 37.5d.

When: t_1 = 0 minutes   (reference section 2.3.3)
     t_2 = 4 minutes
     t_3 = 6 minutes
     t_4 = 8 minutes

     t = 18 minutes

4. $A = 7.7d.$
Where: $m = 1.7d.$ (reference section 2.3.3)
     $n = 4.0d.$
     $p = 0.0d.$
     $r = 2.0d.$
     $u = 0.0d.$ (see section 2.3.3)
     $v = 0.0d.$

     $A = 7.7d.$

5. $Y = T + A$
   $\quad\ = 37.5 + 7.7$
   $\quad\ = 45.2d.$ *or approximately* 3s. 9d.

(b) *The cost to the beneficiary of banking and receipting £3. 10s. 0d.*
   transmitted by bank cheque.

3. $T = \dfrac{46 \times 108.6}{60} + \dfrac{46 \times 16.3}{60}$
   $\quad\ = 95.7d.$

When: $t_1 = 20$ minutes   (reference section 2.3.3)
$\quad\quad\ \ t_2 = \ \ 4$ minutes
$\quad\quad\ \ t_3 = \ \ 6$ minutes
$\quad\quad\ \ t_4 = \ \ 8$ minutes
$\quad\quad\ \ t_5 = \ \ 8$ minutes

$\quad\quad\ \ t = 46$ minutes

4. $A = 21.7d.$

Where: $m = \ \ 1.7d.$ (reference section 2.3.3)
$\quad\quad\ \ \ n = \ \ 3.0d.$
$\quad\quad\ \ \ p = \ \ 0.0d.$
$\quad\quad\ \ \ r = \ \ 2.0d.$
$\quad\quad\ \ \ u = \ \ 0.0d.$ (see section 2.3.3)
$\quad\quad\ \ \ v = 15.0d.$

$\quad\quad\ \ A = 21.7d.$

5. $Y = 95.7 + 21.7$
   $\quad\ = 117.4d.$ *or approximately* 9s. 9d.

The cost to the remitter and beneficiary of transmitting £3. 10s. 0d. by bank cheque is therefore approximately 3s. 9d. and 9s. 9d. respectively, not including bank charges.

The cost of transmitting £3. 10s. 0d. by giro between account holders will be:

(a) For the remitter as follows:

3. $T = \dfrac{9 \times 108.6}{60} + \dfrac{9 \times 16.3}{60}$

   $= 18.7d.$

When: $t_1 = 0$ minutes   (reference section 2.3.3)

$t_2 = 2$ minutes   *Note:* All times can be reduced by at

$t_3 = 3$ minutes   least 50 per cent because all opera-

$t_4 = 4$ minutes   tions are with a pre-printed form and

———————————   confirmation of payment has only

$t = 9$ minutes   48 hours' delay.

4 $A. = 1.8d.$

Where: $m = 0.0d.$ (reference section 2.3.3)

$n = 0.0d.$

$p = 0.0d.$

$r = 1.8d.$ approximately, according to the booklet *The*
   National Giro.

$u = 0.0d.$

$v = 0.0d.$

———————————

$A = 1.8d.$

5. $Y = 18.7 + 1.8$

   $= 20.5d.$ *or approximately* 1*s.* 9*d.*

(b) Cost to the beneficiary.

3. $T = \dfrac{4 \times 108.7}{60} + \dfrac{4 \times 16.3}{60}$

   $= 8.3d.$

Where: $t_1 = 0$ minutes   (reference section 2.3.3)

$t_2 = 0$ minutes

$t_3 = 0$ minutes

$t_4 = 4$ minutes   See note above.

$t_5 = 0$ minutes

———————————

$t = 4$ minutes

4. $A = 0d.$

Where: $m = 0.0d.$ (reference section 2.3.3)

$\qquad n = 0.0d.$

$\qquad p = 0.0d.$

$\qquad r = 0.0d.$

$\qquad u = 0.0d.$

$\qquad v = 0.0d.$

$\qquad A = 0.0d.$

5. $Y = 8.3 + 0$

$\qquad = 8.3d.$ *or approximately* 8d.

If the payment is made by a non-giroist to a giroist, the former has to add the cost of a visit to a Post Office and the fee (9d.) to use a giro inpayment form. If the payment is made by a giroist to a non-giroist, the former is charged the same fee, and the non-giroist has to add the cost of a visit to a Post Office to encash the *payment order* voucher.

But, as shown above, the cost to a giroist remitter and beneficiary of transmitting £3. 10s. 0d. by giro transfer/deposit form is approximately 1s. 8d. for the former and 8d. for the latter, *and there are no bank charges.* In fact, the costs are entirely within the orbit of the two parties concerned to reduce, apart from the amount 1.8d. representing stamp duty.

If we take also the example given in section 2.3.4 of transmitting 4s. 0d. by postal order, we obtain the following comparison of costs:

Transmission method	Amount transferred	Cost of transmission		
		To remitter	To beneficiary	Total
Postal order	4s. 0d.	8s. 8d.	9s. 7d.	18s. 3d.
Bank cheque	£3 10s. 0d.	3s. 9d.	9s. 9d.	13s. 6d.
Giro transfer/ deposit form	£3 10s. 0d.	1s. 9d.	8d.	2s. 5d.

The above figures assume a minimal use of automated office equipment by the remitter and beneficiary. The substitution of mechanised methods should tend to bring office costs down, even with respect to giro methods. Continental firms whose main business is with other giroist firms and individuals find rapid reference is enhanced by prefixing office reference codes with the client's giro account number. As all giro remittance forms bear the account holder's number, this practice facilitates rapid identification if a payment is received without a correspondence reference on it; the *Giro Directory* can be used as an office records guide. For example, a remitter client who omits to put the reference of, say, DH/19767/lh./G on his giro form can easily be traced if his account number of, say, 017 9487 appears as part of the reference: 017 9487/DH/lh./G.

3.7.   Britain's National Giro: Terms of Reference.

On Wednesday afternoon, 21 July 1965, the House of Commons was asked to agree to a motion moved by Mr. Harry Hynd, the Labour Member of Parliament for Accrington: "That this House would welcome the establishment of a postal giro service in the United Kingdom offering similar facilities to those given by postal giro systems in other countries".

At the end of a debate lasting barely 180 minutes, the House agreed without rancour or division to the motion.

In August 1965 a White Paper, *A Post Office Giro*, was published which set out the main objects of the Giro service and the way in which these would function.

A year later, the Directorate of Giro and Remittance Services— a department of the General Post Office—issued a glossy blue covered booklet entitled *The National Giro—The New Current Account Banking Service*. Some 90 000 copies were mailed free to influential people in public utilities, local authorities, trade and professional associations, government departments, and the larger business and commercial institutions, and their comments invited.

In October 1966 a much smaller blue booklet entitled *Giro—
The Modern Banking Service* was distributed by the Directorate
of Giro and Remittance Services through local post offices "in
only six areas in the United Kingdom as a test of public reaction
to Giro proposals". To encourage readers to register their comments a postage-free post card addressed to the Directorate of

Fig. 32. When the Editor of the Swedish Postbankens newspaper *Obs!*
heard that legislation for a British giro service had been agreed by Parliament, he greeted Britain as a newcomer to the world's giro "club" by
printing extracts from the British press reaction to the announcement.
One of the specially drawn illustrations indicating how deeply giro
methods affect the Swedish public was this thumbnail sketch suggesting
that London's famous buskers need no longer depend entirely on pennies
thrown from windows and theatre crowds.

Giro and Remittance Services was inserted in every booklet but,
because there was nothing to hold it in place, quite a few booklets
appear to have been issued without the card. Once it had slipped
out, the reader had neither the publisher's nor the printer's
address to which to direct his observations. Not even a Crown
mark was printed on the booklet to link it with the Post Office
and those who had not actually obtained a booklet at the Post
Office—or had casually picked it up after use by another

person—had no guidance on where to register their reactions. The "six areas in the United Kingdom" were not
named. Some people who inquired at their local library were
directed to send their comments to the author as the writer
of the first book on the subject of Giro. People who inquired for
the publisher's name at the British Museum Copyright Library
were told the booklet was not in the collection as it was a piece
of free literature. It was finally established that the "six areas in
the United Kingdom" were the *English towns* of Swindon, Oldham,
Kettering, Burton-on-Trent, Ipswich, and Weymouth. A few
irritated people took the view that if the Giro Service was to be
run on lines comparable with the lack of attention to detail and
convenience evidenced by the booklet, then the Service was not
worth bothering about.

A critical examination of the principles and proposals published
in August 1965 in the white paper *A Post Office Giro* suggested
that some of the plans outlined in *The National Giro—The New
Current Account Banking Service* and in *Giro—The Modern
Banking Service* appeared to conflict.

The parliamentary motion of 21 July 1965 had called for a
service "offering similar facilities to those given by postal giro
systems in other countries".

During his speech (see pp. 191–6 and 206–7) in Parliament in
support of the motion, the (then) Postmaster-General, Mr.
Anthony Wedgwood Benn, laid heavy emphasis on a giro as a
means of modernising Post Office services.

3.7.1. NATIONAL GIRO PLANS

The plans published in *The National Giro—The New Current
Account Banking Service* and in *Giro—The Modern Banking
Service* followed in broad outline the best pattern of European
countries' giros with several exceptions. In general the plans made
provision for:

1. A Giro Service that would come into operation in 1968.

2. A service operating through a single Clearing Centre, placed to meet the needs of the entire United Kingdom and capable of a 24-hour clearing service. Instructions are to be processed on the day they are received and the resultant new statements of account and confirmation note dispatched the same day.

3. Everyone over 16 years of age will be offered the opportunity to open a business account with a 7-digit number, or a private account with a 9-digit number. The minimum opening deposit is £5 and this may be exhausted to zero but not overdrawn. No interest is paid on balances.

4. The remitter may hand, or send, a payment form to the beneficiary, but no payment will be made until the form is cleared by the Giro Centre. The remitter is responsible for any fraudulent change resulting from direct transmission of a form to the beneficiary.

5. Giro forms can be incorporated in firms' trade literature and stationery to facilitate payments and accountancy, but design must conform to the Giro Authority's requirements.

6. Transfers between giroists will be free and postage will be free.

7. A special Giro Transfer/Inpayment form will enable remitters to make payment through a Post Office or direct through the Clearing Centre. This means, in effect, that a giroist receiving an inpayment form can sign it and then process it like a transfer/deposit form.

8. An automatic debit transfer service enables companies with a large number of debts to collect to do so by asking the Giro Clearing Centre to debit giroists' balances. It will be obligatory for the company to obtain the agreement of the giroist, and to provide the Giro Centre with a form of authority signed by him. The Giro Directorate will hold the company responsible should a payer claim a debit was made without his authority.

9. Companies with a large number of regular giro transactions can obtain statements in computer input form.

10. A standing order service without charge to giroists will be available.

11. A periodic payments service without standing order will help to diminish ancillary paperwork for hire purchase and other firms which collect large numbers of regular payments of varying amounts.

12. There will be special provisions to facilitate the collection of payments from mail order companies' agents.

13. Companies will be able to print special forms to encourage employees to accept wages and salaries by giro. This type of payment can advantageously be negotiated by giro and prove a great saving to the employer, whose wages department will be spared counting out wages in cash. The forms will incorporate payslip details and will be handled confidentially.

14. Employee giroists accepting payment by the above method will be able to draw cash on demand at their local post office to a limit of £20, on payment of 9d. fee. Or they may obtain up to £50 at *any* Post Office after clearance from the Giro Centre, or over £50 at a specified office after clearance from the Centre. This means that wage and salary earners will be able to obtain simple banking facilities at nearly all of Britain's 23 000 sub-post offices and 2000 Crown post offices, throughout the working hours post offices are open, 6 days each week, except for public holidays.

15. Pensions can conveniently be paid by giro with the great advantage to pensioner giroists that they are spared bank charges.

16. There will be no limit to the number of accounts which may be held in the name of one individual.

17. Giroists can pay cash to their own accounts through any post office. Joint stock bank cheques must be sent for clearance direct to the Giro Centre and will take about 4 days to clear.

18. All giro forms will have a space for the remitter to send a message, order, etc., to the beneficiary and no charge will be added for this facility.

19. Payments made by non-giroists to giroists, and vice versa, will be charged a fee of 9d. irrespective of the amount transmitted.

20. Payment orders can be made out to self, or to another person, or a company, and crossed like a cheque for payment into a bank account, or, through a nominated Post Office, in cash to the beneficiary. Alternatively, they may be sent direct to beneficiaries, but are ineffective until forwarded to and cleared by the Giro Centre to the account of the nominee.

21. Giroists can order travellers' cheques and foreign currency by sending a special application to the Giro Centre; the cost is debited to their account.

22. A statement with accompanying documentation (e.g. inpayment or transfer/deposit form credit or debit notification slips, sometimes also called confirmation notes) will be sent to business account giroists each day a change occurs in the balance of their account.

23. Private-account giroists will be sent a statement of account accompanied by documentation as above whenever their balance is credited, or when sufficient debits have accrued to fill one statement sheet, or when 3 months has elapsed since the last statement was issued. A private account holder has the option to request the Giro Centre to supply a statement each day a change is made in his balance.

24. When a transfer is ordered by a giroist from his account to his own or another's joint stock bank account, a fee of 6d. will be charged. The giroist may place a standing order with the Giro Centre to transfer amounts exceeding a specified amount in his account to a joint stock bank account, for example.

25. There is special provision for transfer of funds between a giro account and Post Office Savings Bank and Trustee Savings Bank accounts.

26. Giro directories will be on sale to giroists and the public, and may be referred to at post offices.

27. Giroists will be supplied, by the Directorate of Giro and Remittance Services, with forms and envelopes. A nominal price will be charged and a fee in lieu of stamp duty amounting to approximately 7s. 6d. per fifty forms.

3 7.2. PLANS APPARENTLY IN CONFLICT WITH CONTINENTAL GIRO METHODS

Some of the plans published in *The National Giro—The New Current Account Banking Service* and in *Giro—The Modern Banking Service* appear to conflict with the motion agreed by Parliament on 21 July 1965 and the white paper *A Post Office Giro* (see section 3.7.). The two most inexplicable differences are:

1. That "The minimum transfer allowed will be 5s. 0d."
2. That:

   "A statement of account will be sent to a business holder on every day his balance changes. . . . For private users, a statement will be issued whenever a credit occurs and will include details of any previous debits; additionally, a statement will be dispatched when either sufficient debits have accrued to fill one statement sheet or if three months have elapsed since the issue of the last statement. Alternatively, if he so desires, a private holder may opt specially to receive a statement every day his account balance changes." (*The National Giro—The New Current Account Banking Service*, pp. 13 and 15).

Among the less important seemingly unusual characteristics are the following:

3. The appointment of Messrs. Thomas Cook & Son Limited as agents, with a branch in the Giro Centre, for the issue of travellers' cheques and foreign currency.
4. The difference of treatment offered to business and private account holders, including a 7-digit account number for the former and a 9-digit number for the latter. Also the great length of account numbers with correspondingly great difficulty in memorising them.
5. The high fee charged (9d.) each time a giroist wishes to extract cash from his own account.

It is very likely that many of the seeming inconsistencies will be ironed out after the National Giro gets into its stride. But it would be foolish to try to suppress—as some Members of Parliament

and Post Office officials have attempted to do—the criticism
of what appear to be such wide differences from what the motion
and the white paper promised. Those who have repeatedly implied that criticisms of some of the National Giro plans are based
on fallacies or that the critic had insufficient experience of giro
systems to make his remarks significant, or accused the author,
among others, of basing criticisms on untruths, would do well to
study section 4.4.4 with very great care. He will find evidence in
that section of somewhat strange inaccuracies propagated by Post
Office officials, during the period 1963–4 in particular, which
suggests that even Post Office officials are not infallible. For
example, it will be found that within a few days of taking office a
former Assistant Postmaster-General had data provided to him
which made Parliament believe that the Dutch Giro had made *ten
times* the loss it had actually sustained, and that the French Giro
was run at a loss when the French economy was benefiting from
vast loans at only 1.5 per cent interest. If Post Office officials could
make such errors of judgement in 1963–4, was it not possible
they might make similar errors in 1966–7? Again, those who
would like to have suppressed all criticism of the National Giro
plans were surely making a gross error of judgement themselves.
A controversial subject generates far more public attention than
one cut and dried, and criticism of Post Office plans is likely to have
generated more interest in the National Giro than if everyone had
remained passive and apparently rapt in admiration.

But it is quite true that the number of British people with
sufficient knowledge of giro methods abroad to make useful
criticism of British plans was very small. This position had the
effect of placing a heavier responsibility on those of us with a
personal knowledge of "facilities . . . given by postal giro systems
in other countries"—in the words of the motion—because it
would be so much more difficult to change the National Giro
after operations commenced. Objections were therefore made to
the plans listed above, and apparently in conflict, as follows:

1. The main objection to the 5s. minimum transfer was that it
   would compel giroists to use giro methods and one or more

additional monetary transmission methods—a very untidy arrangement. As the Postmaster-General himself, during the debate on the motion, had called postal orders "very old-fashioned and extremely expensive ways of transmitting money" and had talked of the introduction of a giro against a background of "We contemplate this as a modernisation of our own remittance services . . ."; it had been anticipated that the National Giro would provide a service for the free transfer of all amounts between giroists, just like that of the bulk of continental giros, where the position in the spring of 1966 was:

(a) Countries with no lower limit on free transfers: Austria, Belgium, Denmark, Finland, France, West Germany, Luxembourg, Norway, Lichtenstein, Monaco, San Marino, Sweden.

(b) Countries with a lower limit on free transfers:
  Holland: transfers less than 25 cents forbidden (about 7d.).
  Italy: transfers less than 100 lire forbidden (about 1s. 4d.).
  Switzerland: transfers less than 20 centimes forbidden (about 5d.).

It has been stated that lower limits are placed at a value which would result in no great loss to the remitter if amounts less than this were sent as loose postage stamps. But there is a marked difference between the highest limit of 1s. 4d. and the National Giro's 5s. It surely is a reflection on Britain's reported inability to make a giro pay if transfers less than 5s. were allowed, when so-called "poor" countries like Finland and Norway can afford to offer this inclusive service and still make their giros pay (1968 Exchange rates).

It would have been better if the National Giro had followed Sweden's example, as described in a letter sent to the author on 28 November 1966 by Sweden's Postbanken:

"There are no stipulations concerning the minimum amount of money that can be transferred free between account holders in our giro system.

"If, however, we find that a transfer form is misused by a person sending very small amounts in order only to transmit a written message, we return the form with the information that the giro is not intended to serve such a purpose, but to effect real payments."

In the author's experience the definition of "real" payment can be as little as 75 öre (about 1s. 3d).

Under the paragraph sub-title "Mail Order Business" in the booklet *The National Giro* is the statement: "There will be no cheques and postal orders to bank"; so one is obliged to assume that mail order business for amounts less than 5s. will be impossible.

On 20 January 1967 the Member of Parliament for Moray and Nairn, Mr. Gordon T. C. Campbell, asked the Postmaster-General why a minimum of 5s. on free transfers had been imposed, and the Assistant Postmaster-General replied (*Hansard: House of Commons Debates*, v. 739, no. 126, col. 889):

". . . As to the minimum of 5s. for transfers, market research has demonstrated that there is no public demand for a lower minimum, and many people pay great heed to what market research says. No institutions nor anyone else has objected to a minimum of 5s. per transfer. What kind of payment will companies wish to collect by giro of less than 5s.? Postal orders are widely welcomed for low value payments by the public."

This was similar to the reply given to Mr. Campbell by the Postmaster-General, when he raised this question on 26 October 1966. On 22 February 1967, the Postmaster-General replied (*Hansard: House of Commons Debates*, v. 741, cols. 1859, 1861, 1892):

"With regard to the 5s. minimum which a number of hon. Gentlemen have mentioned, my hon. Friend the Assistant Postmaster-General dealt with this on the Second Reading of the Bill, in column 889. The simple point is that market research has shown that there is no real demand for anything less than the 5s. minimum. But the book makes it clear that these are the conditions we intend to have when we start. When the postal order system finally fades out we may have to look at this again. In the meantime, I think postal orders are adequate for any amounts less than 5s."

Is the defence of the 5s. minimum compatible with the following facts?

1. During the parliamentary debate preceding the agreement to the motion in favour of: "... the establishment of a postal giro service in the United Kingdom offering similar facilities to those given by postal giro systems in other countries," the Postmaster-General spoke of investigations "done with very great thoroughness" by the Post Office and of market research. He gave no hint that the "similar facilities" offered would be so different as to impose a limit, for example, so very much higher than that of Italy—one of the less popular of continental giros. If such investigations had taken place, it must then have been known there would have been this dissimilarity from "facilities . . . given by postal giro systems in other countries". But, be this as it may, the white paper *A Post Office Giro*, published a few days after the Postmaster-General's speech, unambiguously states in section 17: ". . . In addition a giro will provide for everyone cheap facilities for cash remittances of any amount through the Post Office. . . ." Does this agree with the statement "The minimum transfer allowed will be 5s. 0d."?

2. Unless the Government wished the public to believe that the purchasing power of money would be so much devalued by the time the National Giro came into operation that 5s. would be insignificant in value, it surely is a little strange to suggest there would be no demand for the transfer by giro of amounts less than this when all of Britain's European Free Trade Association partners (excepting Portugal, which

has no giro) make adequate provision for the transfer of such small amounts? Are British charities, for example, to be denied the same rights as continental charities to collect the myriads of small contributions which help to swell their funds? No charity appears to have been included in the market survey.

3. It is shown in section 2.3.4 that the lower the value of a postal order the higher the cost of monetary transmission by this method, and that the combination of postage and poundage may amount to anything between 14 and 58 per cent for values less than 5s. Yet this is the method the Postmaster-General commended as "adequate".

4. In March 1967 the Banking Information Service announced that English joint stock bank and Scottish bank account holders would be provided with a free credit transfer service from 1 April 1967. As there is *no minimum transfer limit*, it would appear that the banks' market research findings conflict with the Postmaster-General's claim "that market research has shown that there is no real demand for anything less than the 5s. minimum". A further question by Mr. Gordon Campbell to the PMG disclosed that between 1966 and 1967 the public bought 233 million postal orders for amounts below 5s. Although the PMG claimed earlier "postal orders are widely welcomed for low value payments by the public" (see p. 144), he should know it is a matter of Hobson's choice for the public.

If transfers less than 5s. are uneconomic for the Post Office, could it be that they are trying to get too much profit out of the new service too quickly? To break even and to make a profit of 8 per cent is more than most new enterprises would expect to achieve from the start. Perhaps the authorities ought to consider in greater detail the need to provide a comprehensive service rather than be led by what market surveys suggest the public will just tolerate. There is also the ethical question (dealt with in section 5.1.1) of whether a public service with such capability for promoting economic efficiency and social benefits should be costed on strictly commercial lines?

The objections to the 5s. transfer limit have been given in detail to indicate a number of valid reasons for believing there was a conflict between plans published in *The National Giro* booklet and what had been promised. For brevity, a summary only will be given of objections to the other apparent differences between the plans in the booklet and what had previously been promised.

1. The decision to provide business giroists with a statement of account each day there is a change in their balance—and private account holders are to receive a statement similarly only if they specially opt for the service—seemingly places the responsibility of protecting their accounts from criminal misuse entirely on the shoulders of private account holders, and must leave them to wonder—if they fail to "opt"—how much money is being drained out of their account by automatic debiting operations.

The booklet *Giro—The Modern Banking service* states (p. 10): "With Giro it is important to know how your balance stands as no overdrafts are allowed." and the Government white paper, *A Post Office Giro*, explicitly states (p. 14, section 10): "A credit slip will be sent to each account holder after each deposit or transfer to his account and a statement will be sent to each account holder whenever there is any change in the balance held." It would appear that private account holders will not be given the same service as business account holders, unless they insist—although no distinction between the two is allowed for in the white paper. The Automatic Debit Transfer scheme outlined in the booklet *The National Giro* (p. 4) makes the private account holder who does not exercise his option vulnerable to risk of having his balance raided without warning, and to the point of being overdrawn. The booklet states:

"A company wishing to collect payments in this way will first have to agree with those of its customers who have Giro accounts that they are willing to have their payments automatically debited when due ... Creditor organisations using this facility will have to provide the National Giro Centre with a

form of authority, signed by the account holder against whose
account automatic debit transfers will be made . . . Creditors
will be required to indemnify Giro against the consequences of
transfers initiated by the creditor which contravene any agreement between the parties."

A noteworthy omission is a guaranteed indemnity for trouble, time
and expense a giroist may suffer as a result of his balance being
raided by this means.

When the Member of Parliament for Moray and Nairn, Mr.
Gordon T. C. Campbell, on 20 January 1967, asked the Postmaster-General a question about this seeming departure from
what had been promised in the white paper (*Hansard: House of
Commons Debates*, v. 739, no. 126, cols. 865–6), no public reply
was given, except a reassurance that "The Government are always
prepared to have another look at anything if it is in the interests
of the general public".

2. As Messrs. Thomas Cook & Sons Ltd. is scarcely known
abroad—where British giroists are likely to use their travellers'
cheques—as a British national organisation, there have been
expressions of astonishment at what was considered "an extraordinary attempt by the British Post Office to award a monopolistic privilege to one commercial agency in competition abroad
with other enterprises". In view of the risk of perpetuating this
impression it might have been better if the National Giro's
travellers' cheques had been issued impartially and on the same
lines as, for example, those of the Swiss Post Office Giro. The
Swedish Post Office Bank deals in foreign currency like a commercial bank, so it ought to have been possible—presumably—
for the British Post Office to provide similar facilities without
incorporating the name of a travel agency thought by many people
to be a free-enterprise firm in competition with other free-enterprise firms. Catalogues and other literature issued by Messrs.
Cook do not indicate their nationalised status, so misunderstanding, especially by foreign firms which feel themselves to be
in competition with Cooks, is understandable.

3. No explanation has been offered as to why private account holders should have to use a 9-digit account number. Nearly all continental countries have 6-digit or shorter account numbers. The longer the number the less appropriate it will be as a short-cut to convenience. The author's Swedish postgiro number is 42 78, and, in Italy (with about the same population as Britain), number 1/16941. In Britain it *might* be 3 654 793 or 895 543 865. How cumbersome!

The joint stock banks have stated that if a current account holder maintains a minimum of £50 in his account, he will be allowed up to thirty debitings and creditings per half-year free of charge—meaning he can also write out a cheque to self to obtain cash at the bank. To several potential giroists this facility seems a shade more attractive than having to pay a fee of 9*d*. each time they request a withdrawal of up to £20 from their giro account at their local Post Office. The booklet *The National Giro* detailed on pages 9 and 11 the plans for cash on demand which caused these objections.

Until the Post Office offers a money order service compatible, and capable of being integrated at will, with the National Giro service, it seems the public will have to continue using the most cumbersome and archaic of all monetary transmission systems to bolster up the giro; the postal order. Figure 33 illustrates a Swedish money-order form, typical of those used with the postal service of other giro countries in continental Europe.

3.8. Who Pays for the Giro Service?

One of the most attractive features of the National Giro is that it ought eventually to provide the nation with a source of vast loans at attractively low interest rates. In Sweden, for example, many of the major improvement schemes, such as new towns, roads, bridges, and even educational projects, are cheaply financed from giro-derived loans. Figure 34 shows part of a new suburb of Stockholm built with money from this source.

But as long as the British Post Office is committed to paying an interest rate as high as 8 per cent for loans to modernise its services, there is little chance that the National Giro will make substantial contributions towards the national economy except as a means of reducing public demand for cash and gradually minimising the social problems arising from the circulation of bank-notes and coins.

The "secret" of how the National Giro is financed whilst providing so many free services to giroists has puzzled many people. But the principle is really quite simple and safe.

The Postmaster-General estimated that 1.25 million giro account holders with an average balance of only £100 to £150 would enable the giro to break even *and* provide an 8 per cent return over the long run.

What happens is that giroists are given every encouragement to maintain in their account an amount corresponding to their regular outgoings such as, in the case of private account holders, the amount likely to be required to pay their electricity and gas bills, the telephone account, professional fees and club subscriptions, the television and dog licences, incidental expenses they would normally send by postal order or cheque, gifts and donations, etc.

Neither the joint stock bank account holder nor the giro account holder receives an interest on the amount in his account. But whereas the bank account holder may have to meet bank charges despite the fact that at least some of the money in his account will be invested by the bank for their own profit, the giro account holder has no charges to meet except when he orders transfers to a non-giroist, etc., and the money in his account is invested for the communal benefit of himself and the nation.

There is a continuous interplay of debiting and crediting between giroists, and between giroists and non-giroists, so it would seem the amount in the account of each will not remain the same

FIG. 33. This Swedish money order form is typical of those used by giro countries instead of the British type of money or postal order. Blank forms have no value until completed and handed to the Post Office clerk with the remittance and service fee. The remitter is given a receipt by the Post Office clerk, who then passes the form through the Post Office to the beneficiary. He receives it by the ordinary postal delivery to his address, and can encash it at the nominated Post Office.

INRIKES POSTANVISNING
Mottagardel
Frånskiljes av adressaten

Belopp med siffror
162 kr 50 öre

Avsändarens namn och adress
John Philip
Thomson Street
Fochabers.
Nourland

Meddelande till adressaten
Send the above
sixteen copies
of the " Guide
to European"

INRIKES POSTANVISNING (arkivdel)

Belopp med siffror
162 kr 50 öre

Kronralet med bokstäver, omedelbart åtföljt av ordet "kronor"
One hundred and sixty two kronor &
Adressatens namn
Sven Macdonell & Co. fifty öre
Bostadsadress e. d. (gata, nr, uppg, tr, box, fack etc.)
Chattanvag. 798
Adresspostanstalt
Lund.
LUND POST OFFICE

Redov.-månad	Journalnummer	Redov.-nummer	Sign.	Ankomstni

Giltighetstid: En månad från avstämplingsdagen   Bl 11 (Dec 60)

Plats för frankering
Postanvisning får lyda
på högst 2 000 kr
Får ej utskrivas med
blyerts-, anilin- eller
färgpenna

Meddelande till adressaten
private guest-
houses and
village inns"
at Kr 10:—
each and
Kr 2:50 for
postage and
packing. Also
send me your
latest
catalogue.
J. Philip—.

Obs! Denna mottagardel skall
frånskiljas av adressaten.

	Datum	Tjänsteanteckningar
Omstående belopp kvitteras	/ 19	
Adressatens namnteckning		Legitimationssätt
Budets namnteckning		
Budets adress		Signatur

Kvitto får ej tecknas med blyerts- eller färgpenna.
Der åligger adressaten att legitimera sig. Legiti-
mering sker bäst genom postens identitetskort,
pass eller körkort. Även försäkringsbesked,
skattekort eller likvärdig handling kan efter
postfunktionärens prövning användas som legi-
timation.
Hämtas beloppet genom bud, åligger det budet
att legitimerd sig.

Ankomstdag

Vid efter- eller återsändning
Avsändningsdag   Ankomstdag   Utbetalningsdag

FIG. 33

for long; but the exchange of debitings and creditings tend to even out over a period and to approximate the average; even if an individual private account reaches near exhaustion, it is likely the credit from it has passed to other accounts, and so is not lost to the giro.

The result of all this interplay is that the fluidity requirements of the daily service reaches, on average, a finite figure, and a substantial part of the total credit of all balances is surplus to requirements. This surplus can safely be drained off and offered as a loan at an agreed rate of interest which just balances the cost of running the giro service free of charge to giroists and the Post Office. The loans are always made through or to state-guaranteed organisations, so there is no risk of loss.

But the ultimate success of a giro depends more on the willingness of account holders to understand the principles and to use the service intelligently, than upon the scientifically calculated plan of operation. Any account holder whose conduct produces an exception to the general pattern is likely to attract official action to ensure that non-conformity is not conducted at the expense of other users. A giro is essentially a mass-appeal method so simple and safe to use that risk of error and misunderstanding is unlikely except from the odd mischief-maker. And since the service is run for the benefit of the user and the nation, although many side-advantages accrue, there would have to be a very evil-minded mischief-maker to try and disrupt such a system.

During the parliamentary debate on the motion favouring the establishment of a giro, in the House of Commons on 21 July 1965, the Member for Watford—Mr. Raphael Tuck—described giro as (*Hansard: House of Commons Debates*, v. 716, no. 158, col. 1609):

"... a co-operative measure also, because it provides the means whereby the profit earned by the account holders is shared by the account holders and the nation. The account holders benefit from the many types of free service available

FIG. 34. Typical of the vast public works financed at low interest rates from giro-derived loans is this new suburb of Stockholm, Sweden.

Fig. 34

to them and the nation benefits from access to loans at low rates of interest."

3.9.   The Giroist's World

An indication of the European giroist's world is given in the table of statistics (Table 3) and indicates the magnitude of operations. As international links extend from the National Giro, British industry will increasingly benefit from the direct access to customers in these countries, all of whom are pretty ignorant of British bank cheque and postal order methods but who universally understand giro techniques. Figures are for 1965, the latest available at the time of writing. It will be seen that Britain's EFTA partners had a total of 1 219 000 account holders, and the EEC Group a total of 10 945 000 account holders at a time when Britain was agreeing legislation for the National Giro. And that if the National Giro has 1.25 million account holders, the daily load of transactions, based on the experience of these countries, will average about 1.3 million.

TABLE 3.

Country	Accounts (thousands)	Amounts deposited and withdrawn (£ million)	Transactions (millions)	Total of giroists' balances (£ million)
EFTA				
Austria	137	13 450	261	96.4
Denmark	150	11 000	117	66.2
Norway	77	7870	61	92.0
Sweden	514	44 200	276	234.0
Switzerland	341	25 600	350	315.0
EEC				
Belgium	981	35 820	296	412.0
France	6067	125 000	1095	2450.0
West Germany	2337	64 000	1173	292.0
Holland	1079	21 900	356	300.0
Italy	446	14 400	227	770.0
Luxembourg	35	622	6	10.3

3.9.1. GIRO WORLD STATISTICS

The world of giro countries is shown in black in Fig. 22. Not all countries are nearly as active as those given in Table 3. Many of the former colonial possessions and spheres of influence of Belgium, France, and Holland in Asia and Africa retained their giros after independence and then failed to exploit the latent advantages for a country with a low literacy rate, where a giro could be made a most beneficial self-help instrument of economic improvement.

Table 4 details general facts over a 5-year period as far as replies to questionnaires allow. Read in conjunction with the map in Fig. 22 it will be seen how much Britain, the Commonwealth, and the United States of America have been excluded from a tightly knit, well-integrated financial world with an international monetary language of its own and commonly understood economic principles. But this exclusion was not the fault of giro countries.

TABLE 4.

Country and year giro service started	Giro account holders in thousands, and as a percentage of total population						
	1962	%	1964	%	1965	%	1966–7
1. Algeria (1918)	235	2.1	163	1.5			
2. Austria (1883)	135	1.9	136	2.0	137	2.1	137
3. Belgium (1913)	907	10.0	956	10.3	981	10.6	990
4. Cameroon (1918)			10				
5. Central African Republic (1918)	2						
6. Chad (1918)			See (5) above				
7. China (Formosa)	12	1.2	14	1.3			
8. Congo (Brazzaville) (1913)							

(*continued*)

TABLE 4 (*continued*).

Country and year giro service started	Giro account holders in thousands, and as a percentage of total population						
	1962	%	1964	%	1965	%	1966–7
9. Dahomey (1918)	11	1.8					
10. Denmark (1920)	115	4.0	128	2.8	150	3.2	
11. Faroe Islands (1920)	See (10) above						
12. Finland (1940)	103	2.2	111	2.5	112	2.5	
13. France (1918)	5240	11.0	5801	12.2	6067	12.7	6259
14. Gabon (1918)	See (5) above						
15. East Germany (1908)	159	9.3					
16. West Germany (1908)	2154	3.8	2277	4.0	2337	4.2	
17. Greenland (1920)	See (10) above						
18. Holland (1918)	822	6.9	956	8.0	1079	9.0	1300
19. Indonesia (1918)	0.2						
20. Israel (1953)	11	0.5	13	0.6	14		
21. Italy (1918)	396	0.8	431	0.8	446	0.9	
22. Ivory Coast (1918)	16	0.5					
23. Japan (1906)	500	0.5	441	0.5	434	0.5	
24. South Korea (1918)	0.1						
25. Lichtenstein (1906)	See (39) below						
26. Luxembourg (1911)	31	10.0	33	11.1	35	10.7	
27. Madagascar (1918)	24	0.4					
28. Mali (1918)							
29. Mauritania (1918)							
30. Monaco (1918)	See (13) above						
31. Morocco (1920)	88	7.3	78	6.5	72	6.0	
32. New Caledonia (1918)	3.6	4.5	5.2	5.0			
33. New Guinea (1918)							
34. Niger (1918)	5.0	1.6	8.0	2.0			
35. Norway (1942)	59	1.6	72	1.9	77	2.1	81
36. San Marino (1918)	See (21) above						
37. Senegal (1918)	25	1.2					
38. Sweden (1925)	462	6.1	500	6.6	514	6.8	525
39. Switzerland (1906)	314	5.5	332	5.8	341	5.9	
40. Togoland (1918)	4.4	0.3	6.8	0.4			
41. Tunisia (1918)							
42. United Arab Republic (1918)	0.6		6.2				
43. Upper Volta (1918)	5						
44. Vatican State (1918)	See (21) above						

Of the main giro countries only Morocco and Japan show a serious decline in account holders. The apparent decline in Algeria was caused by separation from France. In Luxembourg the apparent decrease was caused by a shift in the average age of the population and rationalisation of account holdings.

A number of French Polynesian islands are not shown because each is a very small unit by itself.

3.9.2.   GIRO COUNTRIES' INTERNATIONAL PAYMENT AGREEMENTS

Many countries operate international credit transfer services on almost precisely the same pattern as their internal giro service and, because of the well-recognised characteristics of giro, these facilities are much in demand for international trade promotion.

Some years ago, for example, when it was thought that Sweden might join the European Economic Community, it was known that many smaller West German firms planned to make the maximum direct impact on the Swedish public's buying habits by using a combination of this facility and a Stockholm-based giro account.

The listing below indicates the various agreements. Giroists in the country numbered at the left can negotiate credit transfers to the countries listed (and identified for brevity by numbers). This facility has been particularly helpful in maintaining contacts between African countries and Europe. Britain's National Giro makes her an eligible partner in this special financial world. Commonwealth countries who want to join must fulfil the membership rule: establish a giro.

1. Algeria: 2–6, 9, 13–14, 22, 27–32, 34, 37–8, 40–3.
2. Austria: 10, 12–13, 21, 25–6, 35–6, 38–9, 44.
3. Belgium: 1, 8, 10, 12–13, 16, 18, 21, 23, 25, 31, 36, 38–9, 41, 44.
4. Cameroon: 1, 5–6, 9, 13–14, 22, 27–34, 37, 40, 43.
5. Central African Republic: 1, 4, 6, 9, 13–14, 22, 27–34, 37, 40, 43.
6. Chad: 1, 4, 5, 9, 13–14, 22, 27–34, 37, 40, 43.
7. China (Formosa): nil.
8. Congo (Brazzaville): 1, 3.

9. Dahomey: 1, 4–6, 13–14, 22, 27–34, 40–1, 43.
10. Denmark: 1–3, 11, 13, 18, 21, 23, 25–6, 35–6, 38–9, 44.
11. Faroe Islands: 10.
12. Finland: 2, 3, 10, 13, 16, 18, 21, 23, 25, 35–6, 38–9, 44.
13. France: 1–6, 9–10, 12, 14, 16, 18, 21–3, 25–41, 43–4.
14. Gabon: 1, 4–6, 9, 13, 22, 27–32, 34, 37, 40, 43.
15. East Germany: nil.
16. West Germany: 1, 3, 10, 12–13, 18, 21, 23, 25–6, 30–1, 35–6, 38–9, 44.
17. Greenland: 10–11.
18. Holland: 2–3, 10, 12–13, 16, 21, 23, 30–1, 35–6, 38–9, 44.
19. Indonesia: 18.
20. Israel: nil.
21. Italy: 2–3, 10, 12–13, 16, 18, 23, 25, 26, 35–6, 38–9, 44.
22. Ivory Coast: 1, 4–6, 9, 13–14, 27–34, 37, 40, 43, 44.
23. Japan: 2–3, 10, 12–13, 16, 21, 25–6, 31, 35–6, 38–9, 44.
24. South Korea: nil.
25. Lichtenstein: 3–4, 10, 11–12, 16, 18, 21, 23, 26, 31, 35–6, 38–9, 44.
26. Luxembourg: 2–3, 10, 13, 16, 18, 21, 25, 36, 38–9, 44.
27. Madagascar: 1, 4–6, 9, 13–14, 22, 28–32, 34, 37, 40, 43.
28. Mali: 1, 4–6, 9, 13–14, 22, 28–32, 34, 37, 40, 43.
29. Mauritania: 1, 4–6, 9, 13–14, 22, 28, 30–2, 34, 37, 40, 43.
30. Monaco: 1–6, 9–10, 12–14, 16, 18, 21–3, 27–9, 31–2, 34–41, 43–4.
31. Morocco: 1, 3–6, 9–10, 13–14, 16, 17, 22–3, 27–30, 32, 34, 36–44.
32. New Caledonia: 1, 4–6, 9, 12–13, 22, 27–31, 34, 40, 43.
33. New Guinea: 4–6, 9, 13, 27–30, 34, 37, 40, 43.
34. Niger: 1, 4–6, 9, 13–14, 22, 27–32, 37, 40, 43.
35. Norway: 1–3, 10, 12–13, 16, 18, 21, 23, 25–6, 30, 36, 38–9, 44.
36. San Marino: 2–3, 10, 12–13, 16, 18, 21, 23, 25–6, 30, 35–6, 38–9, 44.
37. Senegal: 1, 4–6, 9, 13–14, 22, 27–30, 32, 34, 39, 43.
38. Sweden: 1–3, 10, 12–13, 16, 18, 21, 23, 25–6, 31, 35–6, 39, 44.
39. Switzerland: 2–3, 10, 12–13, 16, 18, 21, 23, 25–6, 31, 35–6, 38, 44.
40. Togoland: 1, 4–6, 9, 13–14, 22, 27–32, 34, 37, 40, 43.
41. Tunisia: 1, 3, 13–14, 30–1.
42. United Arab Republic: 1.
43. Upper Volta: 1, 4–6, 9, 12–13, 22, 27–32, 34, 37, 40.
44. Vatican State: 2–3, 10, 12–13, 16, 18, 21, 23, 25, 30, 35–6, 38–9.

The following countries provide giro facilities for smaller, adjacent countries:

(a) France supplies the giro needs of Monaco.
(b) Italy supplies the giro needs of San Marino and the Vatican State.
(c) Switzerland supplies the giro needs of Lichtenstein.

CHAPTER 4

Giro Guerrilla

ORGANISATIONS and people in British Commonwealth countries, the United States of America, Africa, Asia, and South America have written to suggest that an outline history of the British Giro Campaign would be a helpful guide on how best to shape plans to win a similar innovation for their own country. British students of social and economic history, politics, technology, and business organisation have queried the effectiveness of Parliament's ability to legislate rapidly and competently for a reform as multi-sided as a giro, and have expressed the opinion it ought not to have been entirely placed under the power of one government department to initiate and arrange.

The most successful way to campaign for a giro will vary from one country to another, but there *are* lessons to be learned from British experience. In compiling the following brief history of the British Giro Campaign, I have to record with deep thanks the permission given by several Members of Parliament to reproduce from correspondence with them.

4.1. Lessons for Intending Giro Countries

The long and hard struggle for a British giro service was not, as in some continental countries, the result of action by pressure groups based on chambers of commerce. It was a combination of spasmodic action by a few Members of Parliament over a period of some 55 years, and a private campaign which started in 1946 and concluded with victory in Parliament in 1965.

The struggle was confused, in its early stages in particular, by the arrogance or arrant ignorance of many influential objectors, on one hand, and, on the other, by several enthusiasts who had failed to grasp that a giro is not merely another convenience to graft on to existing Post Office services, but a combination of a banking system entirely different in pattern from anything in the English-speaking world, and an economic and financial institution with extremely broad and powerful effects on numerous facets of national affairs.

The very fact that the few references made in Parliament up to about 1963 were virtually all by Members with Post Office affiliations, had made the public believe "postal cheques"—as giro was called in the House of Commons until about 1961—was a Post Office domestic matter only. This impression was strengthened by the attitude towards inquiries made by any member of the public curious enough to try and find out what the expression meant. General Post Office personnel gave no help; Post Office employees' organisations gave the impression they resented interest by outsiders; the joint stock banks exhibited an extraordinary ignorance, not to be wondered at in view of the fact that they alone probably knew better than anyone how competitive a giro could have been to their chequing services in pre-automation times; and the expression appeared in none but the most expensive dictionaries—and then only very briefly—and in no encyclopedias.

The conspiracy of silence towards the public was so effective that in 1949 a story was going the rounds of some London clubs that:

"Postal Cheques was the immediate postwar code name for a diabolical plan by unrepentant German economists whose plot to wreck Britain's economy consisted of a number of ingenious means of distributing myriads of forged cheques through the post to people named in the telephone directories of the big cities. The unexpected arrival of the various cheques would be explained by an accompanying letter saying that a soldier (not named) killed in the war had left a legacy to the payee, or that a friend (not named) had nominated the payee in a raffle of which the cheque was a prize, etc."

Apparently, this ludicrous story had its origins in the discovery, by somebody who was trying to find out about "postal cheques", that the British Government had examined the German giro in the 1920's and, in 1945–6, members of the Allied Control Commission for Germany had sent a report to London urging British adoption of a system similar to the *Postscheckkonto*.

During the parliamentary debate on the motion in favour of establishing a giro, in the House of Commons on 21 July 1965, the Member for Watford—Mr. Raphael Tuck—emphasised how little the public had been involved in the campaign because of the sparsity of information (*Hansard: House of Commons Debates*. v. 716, no. 158, col. 1604):

"The supporters of a Motion have always been at a disadvantage because of the absence of general knowledge about giro—what it is, what it does, how it operates and how widely it is used, and the financial, economic and social ills that the country suffers as a direct result of not having this public service.

"This lack of knowledge about giro appears to have been nurtured by successive Conservative Administrations. Perhaps to their banking and other free enterprise friends the propagation of information about giro is rather dangerous. We do not know. But the result has been that public pressure to establish a giro service has always been very small."

Whilst discussing the origins of British interest in giro potentials during the same debate, the Member for Brighton, Kemptown— Mr. Dennis Hobden—referred to the emphasis of activity by Post Office personnel (*Hansard: House of Commons Debates*, vol. 716, no. 158, col. 1623):

"I call to mind the action of the Postmaster-General in 1912 in forbidding the then United Kingdom Postal Clerks Association, which was later merged with the Union of Post Office Workers, to conduct a public campaign in favour of introducing a postal cheque and giro system in the Post Office.

"The attitude of the staff was that they wanted the Post Office to give the best possible service to the public and to keep abreast of all the latest developments. But they were forbidden to carry on, on the ground, apparently, that Post Office developments were the business of the Postmaster-General and his administration and the staff must keep to their proper place without interfering."

It has often been claimed that 1912 was the first occasion on which the introduction of a giro was considered by a British Government, but there is evidence that Whitehall was so shocked by the decision, first of Switzerland and then Germany, to adopt Austria's innovation, that a long cool look was taken much earlier than 1912.

4.2. The Development of British Interest in Giro

The Postmaster-General's rebuff of 1912 to his employees was sufficient to bury interest in postal cheques until 5 June 1924 when the first Labour Government, with Ramsay J. Macdonald as Prime Minister, was in power. The Member of Parliament for East Bristol, Mr. Walter J. Baker, had been the Assistant General-Secretary of the Union of Post Office Workers and apparently thought the right Government was in power to introduce the innovation his colleagues of 1912 had failed to win.

The Right Hon. Vernon Hartshorn, then the Postmaster-General, replied (*Hansard: House of Commons Debates*, v. 173, col. 1491):

"This question has often been considered, and it has always been held that there is no considerable scope for a postal cheque system in this country, especially in view of the extent of the banking system and the general use of bank cheques and postal orders for remittance purposes. I see no reason for coming to a different conclusion."

After this rejection by the Labour Government, Mr. Baker did not try again. Perhaps he realised there was much need to educate people into understanding the difference between the postal cheque system and what Britons were accustomed to using.

The next attempt was made by the Member of Parliament for Camberwell, Mr. (later Lord) Charles G. E. Ammon, who had been a Post Office worker for 24 years. On 14 July 1926 he asked the Postmaster-General, by then Sir W. Mitchell Thomson, if he would introduce a postal cheque system.

In the course of his reply the Postmaster-General quoted from a letter sent to Mr. Ammon (*Hansard: House of Commons Reports,* v. 198, cols. 457–8):

"As I promised, I have now looked into the question of postal cheques. I find that the Post Office have investigated this system from 1908 onwards, but have never felt able to recommend its adoption. It is true that certain continental countries have made a success of it. This is partly due to the fact that they run their post offices on cheaper lines than we do and can afford to fix fees for such business on a scale which in our case would result in a heavy loss. But the main reason is that their banking systems are relatively undeveloped, and the postal cheque system has the field more or less to itself. In this country where banking facilities are so widely used and highly developed it is only the smaller and less remunerative accounts which would come to the Post Office. I am advised, therefore, that it would be impossible for us to adopt the system without serious financial loss."

Mr. Ammon was so incensed by this reply that he wrote to continental giro countries and asked: "Is the banking system as highly developed in your country as in England?"

France replied that her banks were superior to the British. Belgium and Germany replied that they considered theirs were at least equal. At the time the postal cheque system in the two latter countries was running at a rate of 36 320 million francs and 78 500 million marks respectively; these are 1925 figures at the currency value of the time, and apparently impressed even the Postmaster-General.

But during the debate noted above, the Assistant Postmaster-General had rather undiplomatically indicated where the Post Office's real interests lay when he arrogantly thundered: "Our banking facilities are immeasurably superior to those of any other country in the world."

Apparently Mr. Ammon did not realise that the analogy between conventional British banking systems and the postal cheque system of the Continent was so slight as to make this remark pointless—for he made no criticism—and the Speaker, if any more knowledgeable on the subject, did not consider it necessary to ask the Post Office spokesman to confine himself to the subject under debate. This reluctance by parliamentary debaters to define postal cheques or giro methods continued right up to the mid-sixties and helped to maintain public apathy. Even as recently as 1967 a senior Post Office official remarked to the author that however imperfect the National Giro plans might eventually prove to be, the main triumph was that progressive planners in the joint stock banks at last could overrule their die-hard and complacent senior executives and shareholders, and get on with the much overdue job of reorganising and modernising Britain's most conservative of industries. This is not the only indication that Post Office personnel are divided in their enthusiasm for a giro and that some, at least, consider it still an obligation to help safeguard the interests of the joint stock banks. Even yet the general public is so ignorant of the full implications of a National Giro as to be unable to dismiss or contradict this type of subversion.

The Post Office Advisory Council had been considering postal cheques from about the mid-twenties whilst both Labour and Conservative Government speakers stalled all pressures for the introduction of the service. In 1928 a member of the General Council of the Trades Union Congress gave evidence in favour of establishing the system but, when finally presented after long delays, the report recorded the Council's opposition. It stated, however: "That in the hope of encouraging a wider expansion of banking habits and economy in currency, a tentative step should be made in the direction of offering cheque facilities for Post Office Savings Bank depositors."

As there had been no sign that the Postmaster-General was making a move to implement the report's recommendations, Mr. Ammon asked on 4 March 1929 when this would take place and was told the matter was still under consideration. Outside observers suggested it would now be appropriate if "the self-interest of Post Office workers to get more work ceased to take so much of Parliament's valuable time".

In 1931 the Post Office introduced a system whereby withdrawals from the Post Office Savings Bank could be used to pay third parties by way of draft warrants, and the few members of the public who had heard of, or had taken an interest in the postal cheque controversy, thought that at long last the Postmaster-General had conceded to demands, and the result was not so very exciting after all.

4.3. Schoolboy International Adventuring

This was the position in 1931 when, as the schoolboy winner of a prize for an essay on the Life and Work of Dr. Fridtjof Nansen, the Arctic explorer and exponent of refugee resettlement, I was sent to Geneva to study the League of Nations (the inter-war equivalent of the United Nations Organisation) and its agencies. In those days the school journey party movement had not started and the rarity of a British schoolboy in Geneva had the effect of opening many doors. I was fortunate in making contact with officials of the International Labour Office—the LON's centre for study and advice on workers' conditions—and I came into contact with several officials enthusiastically knowledgeable about the postal cheque system and its likely long-term beneficial effects on the national economics of industrial and developing nations and, in particular, its possibilities for workers' savings movement improvement.

It was urged on me to regard the postal cheque system as something entirely different from anything we had in Britain and as a subject worthy of careful study divorced from Post Office affairs, for its main importance lay in its impact on business and social organisation in the countries where it had proved most beneficial; that was in Switzerland, Germany, France, Belgium, and Sweden.

I was given a typographically drab document printed in French on poor paper, and was told it contained all the information I would need until I could consult the information sources "undoubtedly available in London libraries". But on returning to Britain I found there was not only the conspiracy of silence outlined previously, but public libraries were no help.

Whilst studying communication engineering after leaving school I worked with systems like the Creed perforated-tape transmitter, and came to the conclusion that a sophistication of the equipment would soon do more than merely transmit morse at high speed; that it comprised the basic ingredients for the partial mechanisation of post giro processes.

Rather than become a "Sparks" on some ocean-going vessel, I went on to be a student engineer engaged on television picture transmission research during the stimulating early days of pulsed-circuit invention—when the foundations for so many later inventions such as radar and electronically operated computers were laid. What I had seen in Switzerland of the postal cheque system and the experience I had gained of the French and Belgian methods on summer holiday visits to those countries had convinced me that one day the technologies in which Britain was then taking the lead would very probably be applied to postal cheque methods, to make these principles even more efficient.

4.4.   The British Giro Campaign Opens

War-time work with European Resistance Movement personnel and with refugees from German invasion in Holland, France, Denmark, Norway, etc., helped to build up a comprehensive picture of the impact of giro methods on business activities well beyond the advantages to the Post Office, and made it obvious that an essential prerequisite for success of any campaign in Britain was a need to extend a knowledge of giro beyond Post Office personnel.

Nearly 3 years' sojourn in Denmark and Sweden, from the end of 1946, enabled me to obtain much-needed experience of giro methods in practice, and to study the effect on many aspects of business organisation. It seemed that British people in the past had very much underestimated the effect of monetary transmission methods in terms of office administration costs, and there was need to concentrate publicity on this side of a giro. One of my tasks in Sweden was to instruct Scandinavian Airline Service personnel in English aviation terminology. Many of the flight engineers and navigators had flown with the Royal Air Force during the war, and it was very useful to hear their candid comments on British bank cheques and postal and money orders. I was often reminded that both Norway and Finland had managed to introduce the efficiency-promoting giro system in mid-war, and that the British could have done so, too, if they had wanted to.

4.4.1.   Too Esoteric for Parliament!

All attempts to persuade Members of Parliament of the first and second postwar Labour governments that they ought—then—to lay the foundation for Britain's future by putting a giro at the top of their list of legislative urgencies proved abortive. The few with an understanding of what a giro implied said it was too esoteric to capture the imagination of the House of Commons; that there was so much more in the public eye, like the need to reform health, insurance, and education, and to arrange for steel nationalisation, and they could not neglect the attention of clamouring lobbyists. Nor was help to be found among organisations one might have expected to be sympathetic; they were so much taken up with problems of demobilisation and retraining men and women from the Forces, and in finding new offices in London after war-time evacuation; nobody was interested in anything as strange as a giro. And the idea of a major upheaval in monetary or banking methods was quite enough to put off many people tired—too tired—of the upheavals caused by the war and the change to peace. Members of Parliament were so overworked and fatigued by make-do conditions that they asked me to stop worrying them. Others curtly drew my attention to the Post Office Savings Bank warrant innovation of 1931, and demanded I should digest that part of *Hansard*.

Obviously, the muddle between postal cheques, the POSB warrant scheme, and giro would continue as long as no written material indicated the true position. So, revising a leaflet I had written and published in 1946 entitled *Postal Cheques Are Your Business*, I enlarged it under the title of *Giro—Europe's Wonder Bank*. During 1951–2 some 500 to 1000 copies were sold at 6d. each from a house in Grosvenor Road, Godalming, Surrey, and were ordered as much by continentals as by British people; the former were interested because this was the first explanation, against a giro background, of the British monetary transmission system and important knowledge for continentals who were trying to forge postwar trading links with Britain.

Armed with some of these pamphlets I called on a Member of Parliament and was asked what had been the reaction of the newspapers—his barometer of public enthusiasm. When I called on journalists for their support, they referred to the *Hansard Index* to see how parliamentarians had reacted. The result, of course, was that the one waited for the other and nothing happened. But one personally sympathetic journalist whose war-time duties had brought him into contact with German and French giro working said he would gladly have written a leader article if he did not fear reprisals by banking interests, on the one hand and, on the other, by his editor, who would say the subject was above the level of popular public interest. As I left his office he quipped; "You'll find it hard to reform British Banking from a bedsitter in Golders Green!" He was one of the few who understood why I was winning the unenviable reputation of being either an anarchist or a communist bent on blasting Britain's financial institutions, and why it was useless to refer people with such wild ideas to the fact that every progressive country in western Europe, except the United Kingdom, had a giro. Postwar Britain was suffering from a surfeit of self-glory and little on the Continent was as good as we had it here. If a giro had been established at the time of postwar reorganisation the cost of reconstruction of our economy would have been immeasurably eased.

My next move was to establish a working model of giro opportunities and methods, from a British address, to demonstrate to sceptics the advantages of the system. As it required no licence to export newspapers, magazines, and books, and custom formalities were minimal, I set up a direct mail book export and subscription agency as a spare-time hobby and, in particular, intensively marketed a small magazine, *English Illustrated* (Fig. 35), which I had founded in 1949 in association with one of the university presses. The magazine was designed to stimulate interest in the use of English learned by continental youth at their school desks, and was mailed to them direct from London each month, thereby giving them a sense of close contact with the country whose language was being learned. The packet of *English Illustrated* copies arriving, for example, in a remote Sicilian town school, with English stamps on the wrapper, proved an immensely popular way of emphasising the use of the language as opposed to the theoretical need for it according to the school examination syllabus. The fact that I was using identically the same way to gather subscriptions as the local journal publishers made it all the more acceptable to teachers. *English Illustrated* was the first foreign journal officially allowed in the state schools of many foreign countries. Over 95 per cent of all copies printed were exported during the 12 years publication continued and, at the time it was stopped in 1961, there were subscribers in more than eighty-five countries.

4.4.2. BRITAIN'S FIRST GIRO-OPERATED AGENCY

Initial attempts to obtain a giro account operated from a British address were not always successful and involved visits to giro authorities in several countries to iron out legal objections.

On 19 August 1954 the first account was opened, and was Swedish postgiro number 44 18. This was followed in September by Danish giro account number 10 439 and in December by Dutch giro account number 145 703. By mid-1956 I had arrangements in Norway, Belgium, Luxembourg, West Germany, Austria, Switzerland, and Italy and had distributed some 20 000 copies of a sales pamphlet to selected addresses. Most of the existing and former colonial possessions of Belgium, France, etc., were included in the giro account arrangement, so most of continental Europe, Africa, and much of Asia was my oyster.

But in mid-1956 a tussle developed with the British Customs and Excise authorities, who tried to extract purchase tax on the giro inpayment forms I wanted to import and overprint with the titles and subscription particulars of British newspapers and periodicals. But, at long last, on 30 August 1956 a letter arrived granting:

"... as a concession the Giro forms in question will be admitted without payment of Purchase Tax provided the forms are used solely in connection with the exportation of British periodicals and books and that none is retained permanently in the United Kingdom."

What other use could be made of giro inpayment forms printed for use with Continental giros only the Customs authorities could

---

FIG. 35. *English Illustrated* was the first British periodical bearing instructions on how to render subscriptions direct to the United Kingdom by postal cheque, and carried, from about 1954 onwards, giro account numbers to facilitate payments from readers in Europe, Africa, and Asia.

THE ENGLISH LANGUAGE LEARNER'S FIRST MAGAZINE

ENGLISH Illustrated

OCTOBER, 1954
Vol. V. No. 8.

BELGIUM & LUXEM'G	1 yr : 60 Frs.	
*12 plus : 50 Frs.	100 plus : 35 Frs.	
DENMARK	1 year : Kr. 8:00	
*12 plus : Kr. 6:50	100 plus : Kr. 4.75	
FINLAND	1 year : 300 Mk.	
*12 plus : 260 Mk.	100 plus : 225 Mk.	
FRANCE & MOROCCO	1 yr : Frs. 375	
*12 plus : Frs. 320	100 plus : Frs. 230	
GERMANY	1 year : 4.75 Mks.	
*12 plus : 3.90 Mks.	100 plus : 2.75 Mks.	
HOLLAND	1 year : fl. 4.50	
*12 plus : fl. 3.50	100 plus : fl. 2.50	
ITALY	1 year : 700 L.	
*12 plus : 575 L.	100 plus : 400 L.	
NORWAY	1 year : Kr. 8:00	
*20 plus : Kr. 6:50	100 plus : Kr. 4.75	
PORTUGAL	1 year : 32$00	
130 plus : 20$00		
SPAIN 26$00	1 year : 60 ptas.	
100 plus : 40 ptas.		
SWEDEN 50 ptas.	1 year : Kr. 6:00	
*12 plus : Kr. 4.50	100 plus : Kr. 3:50	
SWITZERLAND	1 year : 5 Frs.	
*12 plus : 4 Frs.	100 plus : 3 Frs.	

THE PURPOSE of English Illustrated is to help all, but specially beginners and young people, to enjoy learning English and make adventurous use of their knowledge. This typical British monthly picture newspaper has items graded in difficulty to suit the ability of people who have learnt English 1-4 years. Hard words are explained, where necessary, in a glossary. This topical and stimulating supplement to studies is an essential introduction to English and the ideal way to make practical use of lessons.

TURKEY	1 year : TL. 4.50	
*12 plus : TL. 3.75	100 plus : TL. 2.75	
YUGOSLAVIA	1 year : 350 Din.	
*12 plus : 300 Din.	100 plus : 200 Din.	

POSTAGE INCLUDED. *Cost each Group Subscription when 12 (or 20) or more are ordered together : 1 FREE SUBSCRIPTION given to person sending each order. PUBLISHED monthly except July and August. See page 12 for more prices and Agents' addresses.

WHERE TO SEND ORDERS & PAYMENT

★ If you pay by post cheque, be sure you write the payment is for :—

"ENGLISH ILLUSTRATED"

—and give the month your subscription is to start.

AUSTRIA: Journals & Books in English. ★Scheckkonto Nr. 28.184, P.O. Box 113, 60 Market St., Watford, Herts, England.
BELGIUM & LUXEMBOURG: English Illustrated, c/o Westminster Foreign Bank Ltd., ★C.C.P. 132.57, 2-4 Treurenberg, Bruxelles.
DENMARK: English Illustrated postkonto Aarhus 49.51.
FINLAND: (1) Akateeminen Kirjakauppa Oy, Keskuskatu 2, Helsinki. (2) Rautatiekirjakauppa Oy. ★Postisiirtotili 6000. Helsinki.
FRANCE: English Illustrated C.C.P. Paris No. 947, Credit Lyonnais, 19 Bld. des Italiens, Paris. Ecrit pour mandat: "Pour le credit du compte 502—690.00 de English Illustrated suivant autorisation de l'Office des Changes No. 1, 223,940 du 8 aout 1953."
GERMANY: Journals & Books in English. ★Postschekkonto Hamburg Nr. 400034, P.O. Box 113, 60 Market St., Watford, Herts, England.
GREECE: (1) Linguaphone Institute, 10 University Street, Athens. (2) Any bookshop.
HOLLAND: English Illustrated postrekening 145703, P.O. Box 113, 60 Market St., Watford, Herts, England.
ICELAND: Snaebjorn Jonsson & Co. Ltd., The English Bookshop, Hafnarstraeti 9, Reykjavik.
INDIA: (1) By money order direct through a post office. (2) Linguaphone Institute Ltd., 359 Hornby Road, Bombay.
ITALY: Banco di Napoli, Parliamento 2, Roma. ★C/C postale N. 1/2686. Write in Italian on the C/C postale payment form: "For the credit of ENGLISH ILLUSTRATED Account Port/Estero/Ita, P.O. Box 113, 60 Market St., Watford, Herts, England."
NORWAY: English Illustrated ul. loro, Den norske Creditbank, ★Postgiro 9100, Postboks 765, Oslo.
PORTUGAL: (1) Linguaphone Institute, Lauria 98, BARCELONA. (2) Banco Lisboa & Acores, Rua Aurea 88, Lisboa.
SPAIN: (1) Linguaphone Institute, Lauria 98, BARCELONA. (2) Editore Alhambra SA, Claudio Coello 76, Madrid.
SWEDEN: English Illustrated postgiro 41418, P.O. Box 113, 60 Market Street, Watford, Herts, England. ★C.C.P. Berne III 19503.
YUGOSLAVIA: Jugoslovenska Knjiga, Terazie, Beograd.
TURKEY: Pay by Unesco Book Coupon purchased at: Bibliotheque Nationale (Milli Kutuphane), Ankara.

FIG. 35

imagine. Nevertheless, they withdrew this "concession" without warning or explanation in 1962.

The next move was to interest newspaper and periodical publishers in these opportunities for subscription promotion, and I was given some kindly help in this by officers of the Periodical Proprietors Association. The term *giro* proved so confusing—many associated it with a compass—that I dubbed inpayment forms "cardslips" and, opened a direct mail campaign with the object of winning a good return on 1956–7 subscriptions. Several proprietors of technical and general periodicals took cardslips and undertook their own promotion by sending out invitations to existing and lapsed subscribers, and were quite astonished when the response proved the benefit of approaching Italians and Frenchmen, Germans and Danes, etc., in this way. For example, during approximately the last 5 years of publication of the *King-Hall News-Letter* many of their continental subscribers paid by cardslip. Although the cardslip scheme and the British Giro Campaign were mutually self-supporting and relieved me of considerable expense, and proved rewarding in persuading people that giro was not just a theoretical idea, some £15,000 of my personal resources had been sunk in the campaign by the time of victory.

It has been suggested several times that I committed commercial suicide by publishing so much about the benefits of a giro. This is entirely true. An expert knowledge of how to exploit the continental giro system for personal gain was indeed valuable. But I felt that other issues had to be considered. I had not set up a giro network as a full-time job in export promotion; the original intention was to provide proof for British sceptics that this was a viable system we ought to have in Britain, and one which would very much benefit our growing interest nationally in computer utilisation. But I was often tempted to keep this excellent trade secret to myself.

In seeking information globally on Post Office administrations' views on giro methods, I found there was a market for a book in English that would educate government officials and others in countries without giros. In particular, countries in South America and where the native language was Portuguese or Spanish sought this help.

4.4.3.   A LONE CAMPAIGN

A search for collaborators to share the cost and organisation of a giro campaign met with a poor response. A letter dated 12 May 1958, from the General Post Office, London, referred me for information to a book published in 1911 and the annual accounts, and then went on to suggest I might like to send my book manuscript to them to check for accuracy!

A letter dated 10 June 1958 from the London offices of the journal *The Economist* stated that they had published nothing about giro with the exception of an article in one of their issues of November 1957.

On 13 June 1958 the Secretary of the Research and Economics Department of the Trades Union Congress wrote:

> ". . . the Trades Union Congress in 1926 adopted a resolution in favour of the Postal Cheque System and subsequently a member of the General Council, Mr. W. J. Bowen, gave evidence on behalf of the TUC to the Committee of the Post Office Advisory Council, which reported in 1928 on the question of instituting a Postal Cheque System.
>
> "The Trades Union Congress has not since given any further consideration to this matter."

On 15 December 1958 an official of the Union of Post Office Workers wrote:

> "I am afraid I am not able to help you in regard to the attitude of the Union on the Postal Cheque System because we have made no declaration on this subject since 1928, when the matter came before a Royal Commission."

Despite approaches I made to national organisations and to individuals with the object of finding others to share the cost and responsibility of the Giro Campaign, which was burdensome and often extremely discouraging, I obtained practically no assistance. Many people remarked that one man could not hope to change banking habits or must be eccentric to make the effort. Extensive research over the years disclosed that my library of giro literature was the largest on this subject in the United Kingdom and so, with the experience of promoting subscriptions to British periodicals through the continental giros, I felt in a strong position to argue the merits of a giro for Britain and made it known I was prepared to talk to any group that would give me 30 minutes of their time.

The Industrial Bankers' Association (amalgamated with the Finance Houses Association in 1966) was probably the first organisation to take a creative interest in the Giro Campaign. A recent letter from the National Federation of Sub-Postmasters indicates that their interest was aroused slightly later. The former body's *Annual Report*, dated 16 May 1962, contains the following:

"In July 1957 the Association approached the Postmaster-General with the suggestion that there should be set up a new transfer system on the lines of the giro system which is operated in many Continental countries. In November 1959 the Association was advised that the whole matter was being re-examined in the Post Office in connection with the recommendation of the Radcliffe Committee. The Association was informed that a great deal of information about various transfer systems had already been collected and was now being digested. In August 1960 the Postmaster General advised the Association that the results of the Post Office enquiry into the new transfer system and the questions arising were being considered at Government level. This consideration had led to the need for further enquiries which were then being pursued.

"In the Spring of 1961 it was reported that the Postmaster General, when addressing the Annual Conference of the National Federation of Sub-Postmasters at Clacton, said that he felt strongly that the Post Office should embark upon a giro system. In the House of Commons on 20th February, 1962 the

Postmaster General was asked why a decision regarding the introduction of the giro system into the Post Office had been so long delayed and whether he would regard the matter as one of urgency. The Postmaster General replied that the subject required careful consideration from many angles, but he would make a statement as soon as he could.

"As it is now nearly five years since the Association first raised this matter with the Post Office one clearly cannot deny that the matter is receiving careful consideration. Perhaps it is not unreasonable to suggest that the time for action is fast approaching, particularly in view of the fact that the United Kingdom may shortly be entering the European Common Market, where such systems have been in wide-spread use for many years."

4.4.4. Official Action Begins

The first signs of official recognition that giro was something more than merely a convenience to graft on to Post Office services came with the publication in August 1959 of the Report of the Radcliffe Committee on the Working of the Monetary System. Paragraphs 953–64 outlined the system as an alternative to the services of joint stock banks. The concluding paragraph stated:

"We consider that, in the absence of an early move on the part of existing institutions to provide the services which will cater for the need we have in mind, there would be a case for investigating the possibility of instituting a "giro" system to be operated by the Post Office. This investigation would have to make some assessment of the demand for, and likely use and growth of, such a system, the technical and practical problems of entrusting the operation of the system of the Post Office, and the possibility of co-operation with the joint stock banks and savings banks; in all these matters it would be necessary to take full account of continental experience."

The "need we have in mind" was summed up in the opening sentence of paragraph 957:

"There is some evidence for thinking that there is some demand for a simple transfer service, without the ancillary services which the banks offer to their customers."

The report made no comment on the wider effects of a giro, such as business efficiency enhancement, the lessened opportunities for crime involving money, and the beneficial impact on social habits of the public, and therefore, in my view, had failed to draw attention to the full impact a British giro might have on the national economy. It is a truism that when money is efficiently applied the economy is improved; continental giros had demonstrated this principle in high degree and, to ensure that these aspects of giro were adequately brought to public attention, the book I had completed and was seeking a publisher for was withdrawn and enlarged to emphasise this side of a giro; I also attempted to include additional information to give the "full account of continental experience" demanded by the report.

As publishers were still uninterested, I approached organisations which might give limited publicity, such as Political and Economic Planning, which considered the idea of producing a broadsheet on the subject, but wrote to me on 11 September 1962 that their Committee ". . . realise that the system would have considerable advantages but feel that it is rather too technical a subject for treatment by PEP."

The Institute of Economic Affairs wanted to publish a study of "some 12 500 words" and stated that the papers I had submitted "would need fairly extensive editorial treatment". On consideration I found it would be impossible to condense a hard-hitting treatise on the case for a British giro into such a small wordage.

From 1960 onwards interest among Members of Parliament was beginning to show for the first time since the 1930's. On 1 June 1960 the Opposition speaker on Post Office affairs—Mr. Roy Mason—had asked the Postmaster-General, the Right Hon.

Reginald Bevins (*Hansard: House of Commons Debates*, v. 624, col. 139):

> "To what extent he had given consideration to the introduction of a postal cheque system in British post offices, and if he will make a statement.
>
> "Mr. Bevins: I am not yet able to make any statement, but I hope to be ready soon after the recess."

But time passed, and there was no sign of action, and one got the impression the Government was adopting the same sort of delaying tactics as its predecessor had done between 1924 and 1929.

But, surprisingly perhaps, one of the next questions came from the Conservative Member for Taunton, Mr. Edward du Cann, who wanted to know (*Hansard: House of Commons Debates*, 29 March 1961, v. 637, col. 136):

> ". . . what conclusions he [the Postmaster-General] had reached as a result of his study of the possibilities of the introduction of a Giro system into the operation of the General Post Office following recommendations of the Radcliffe Committee, and if he will now make a statement.
>
> "Mr. Bevins: I am still pursuing the matter, but am not yet ready to make a statement."

After the announcement in 1961 that the joint stock banks had introduced a credit transfer service—which was a thinly veiled attempt to forestall a giro by catering for the "need" mentioned in the report of the Committee on the Working of the Monetary System—this question seemed rather theoretical.

Among the Members emerging with a keen interest in giro was the late W. R. Williams, the Member for Openshaw, another former Post Office employee. In a letter dated 27 February 1963, and written shortly before his death, he said:

> "I have been interested in this matter for the best part of five years and the reason why I put my name down for the

Adjournment Debate is that I am getting very anxious and concerned at the delay on the part of the Postmaster General in reaching a decision on the subject."

This debate was the first considerable airing giro had received in Parliament since the 1920's, and Mr. Williams pulled no punches in showing where blame lay for the continuing inactivity in reaching a decision. He described the beneficial effects produced by the impartial assessment by the Committee on the Working of the Monetary System, and asked (*Hansard: House of Commons Debates*, 4 March 1963, col. 167):

"What has happened since then? On 30th September, 1959, the then Director-General of the Post Office informed the Post Office Department Whitley Council that the matter was under close examination. He said that while it would be too early to prognosticate on what branch of the Post Office would develop the new system, he would seek to ensure that if the Giro system was introduced it would be as a Post Office service. It is almost inconceivable to believe that that item is still on the agenda of the Departmental Whitley Council today; still under 'inactive' consideration."

The Assistant Postmaster-General, Mr. Ray Mawby, had taken office less than a week earlier but was responsible for putting the Government's attitude in this 30-minute debate that turned out to be so crucial. He rejected the proposal for a giro on the grounds it would cost too much, and could not be grafted on to the existing Savings Bank. The future of giro looked dead, indeed.

Still without a publisher for the book I had withdrawn from offer to revise and enlarge to more nearly meet the information requirements outlined in the report of the Committee on the Working of the Monetary System, I now again revised it to include some rather startling findings. Following up several of the claims made by the Government in the adjournment debate, I found it difficult to believe the statement: ". . . for example, to the best of our knowledge, neither the French nor the German system pays."

In reply to a copy of this claim sent to the French giro authority, I received a letter vindicating their system's economics and showing how much the French Treasury benefited from massive loans at very low interest as a direct result of giro operation. This letter eventually appeared on page 194 of *Giro Credit Transfer Systems* and, I have been told, did much to dissuade the Conservatives in Opposition from putting up a tough fight against the establishment of Britain's giro. I found other claims, too, which shrivelled under investigation. But the most monstrous was yet to come. It was that, in January 1964, during the debate on the Post Office Borrowing Powers Bill, the Assistant Postmaster-General claimed the Dutch giro made a loss of nearly £300 000 in 1962.

A letter from the Director-in-Chief of Financial and Economic Affairs of the Netherlands Postal and Telecommunications Services, dated 11 January 1965 stated:

> "I trust that these annual reports will produce ample and reliable proof that the statement of a loss of £300 000 in 1962 is incorrect. Most probably there has been a misquotation of the currency unit, viz. the loss in 1962 was actually Dutch florin fl. 300 000 or approx. £30 000 and not £300 000."

The reports were printed in excellent English, so there is little excuse for the General Post Office to have got its arithmetic wrong by a factor of 10. I am now convinced Mr. Mawby was given inaccurate information by his advisers.

By mid-1963 signs were beginning to appear of a rapidly growing interest in giro campaigning and I again went in search of a book publisher, with the same result as before. Being aware now that I had information vital to disseminate in advance of any further attempts to establish giro, I started to set the text by typewriter for reproduction by offset lithography, and then Pergamon Press agreed to take this work in advance of the book I had been preparing on my own branch of technology.

Believing this to be a now-or-never opportunity to publicise the case for a giro widely, I resigned from professional work for a year to give the Campaign the time it needed and also to revise the book

manuscript again, to turn it into a hard-hitting campaign document which was likely to influence government officials, etc.,
throughout the British Commonwealth. Again, questionnaires
were sent to every giro country, and replies in some ten languages
were translated, the results analysed and documented. It was no
light task for the author of a first book.

Meanwhile, influential bodies were starting to take notice and
reactionary elements were obviously starting to be apprehensive.
It was no secret I was preparing a book that would be hard-
hitting and several attempts were made to get a sight of some of
its pages before publication; for example, the dustbin at my home
was searched several times by visitors who came by night and
removed all the torn scraps of rejected copy. Discovering this,
I deliberately placed some bogus papers in the dustbin, suggesting
the United States of America was about to introduce a giro. An
unknown voice from a non-existent number telephoned a week
later to inquire the source of my information.

On 16 October 1963 a letter arrived from Mr. Roy Mason,
M.P. who, since the death of W. R. Williams, M.P., was the
(then) Opposition's speaker on Post Office affairs. He wrote:

> "I can quite safely state there has been no official Labour
> Party pronouncement on the introduction of a Giro system in
> this country. I cannot tell you whether the Party has in mind
> setting up a Study Group to investigate the best way of estab-
> lishing such a system.
>
> "As no doubt you are aware, apart from one or two questions
> in the House and an adjournment debate by my late friend, this
> matter has not been raised much in the House of Commons at
> all.
>
> "Perhaps you would contact me again within a week of the
> House reassembling so that I might have talks with our Leaders
> on this matter and then be able to more fully inform you of our
> intentions."

On 17 October 1963 a letter came from the Right Hon. Douglas
Jay, P.C., M.P.:

"Many thanks for your letter of October 8 about the Post Office Giro system. I am strongly in favour of this, and I think there is a strong case for a campaign on the subject. I will have a word with one or two of my colleagues about it, and let you know their reactions."

A letter written by Anthony Wedgwood Benn, M.P., dated 12 November 1963, inquired:

"If you have, in writing, a layman's guide to what Giro is and how it works, I shall be most interested to see it. Perhaps later we could have a talk about it."

A general election was due in 1964 and the concensus of opinion pointed to June as the time. Having suffered bitter dis-illusionment when the first and second postwar Labour Government's supporters disclaimed interest in giro legislation, I concen-trated, in the months preceding the election, as much time as I could manage in making contact with as many Members of Parliament as I could reach. Fortunately, the election was even-tually delayed until October, which allowed time for my book—the first in the English language on the subject—*Giro Credit Transfer Systems* to be published just before the election and, in view of the kindness of the Right Hon. Douglas Jay, P.C., M.P., in writing a foreword for it, had the effect of concentrating more public attention on giro than ever previously. But even at that stage, most politicians seemed to regard early legislation as extremely unlikely.

But, to return to the gradual development of an official cam-paign, it is worth quoting from another letter from Anthony Wedgwood Benn, M.P., for it shows how, from January 1964, the stage was being set for the Labour Party's return to power:

"The points you make are most interesting and I think will have considerable bearing on the policy a Labour Government follows after the election. It is unlikely we shall be discussing this again before the election but the Labour Party has now gone beyond the point of organising debates and it is now planning what it will do when it comes to power. It is here I think your expertise would be most useful."

A further letter from the Right Hon. Douglas Jay, P.C., M.P., suggested the Parliamentary Labour Party was starting to take a good look at every aspect of a giro. He wrote, on 7 February 1964:

"I am most interested that your guide on the subject is going to the publisher and should be very glad to know when it is available for study."

In April the news broke that the Government was proposing to move the Post Office Savings Bank from Kensington, in West London, to Glasgow, Scotland. There appeared to me to be two good reasons why this should not happen:

1. There would be an everlasting muddle between Britain's first trustee savings bank to introduce a giro-like service (described on pp. 47–9 and 203 of *Giro Credit Transfer Systems*), and the Post Office Savings Bank. The former bank, the Savings Bank of Glasgow, had been in the City since 1836.
2. Continental experience suggested the essentiality of siting a Giro Clearing Centre adjacent to the Post Office Savings Bank. Glasgow did not appear central enough for the rapid communications with the rest of the United Kingdom the giro would need.

On the request of Mr. Anthony Wedgwood Benn I drew up a report to outline the disadvantages but, surprisingly, when the Labour Party came to power, nothing was done to alter the former Government's decision.

The first indication that the Parliamentary Labour Party had decided to legislate for a giro came in a letter written on 21 April 1964 by the Right Hon. Richard H. S. Crossman:

"Thank you for your letter of April 9th about the Giro System, in which you reminded me of Sir Frank Soskice's admirable speech on behalf of the Labour Opposition in favour of it last

December. I can assure you that this speech represents party policy and we are strongly in favour of the system.

"Let us hope that the Pergamon Press book will get some of the facts across more widely."

To build up a body of informed opinion which could become the pressure group if the Labour Party was returned to power after the election, I canvassed support for a working party consultative committee but received lukewarm support. A letter dated 13 May 1964 from Mr. Roy Mason indicated the true level of support that might, after all, be forthcoming:

"I am not fully convinced that there is a need for a working party or a study group to formulate details for a British Giro System. Whilst the Party is favourable to the idea, it would not be in the priority list for immediate legislation if we came to office.

"However, I will have words with some of my colleagues who are interested in this subject to see whether they would think it worth while and would devote some time to studying the formulation of a Giro plan."

The suggestion of low priority was exactly the impression I had been given whilst talking to officials in Labour Party Headquarters and it seemed to me that if the country's economic position was as critical as initial election literature was suggesting, it would be folly for the Government returned to power to baulk the giro question for long.

The only way to keep alive this newly awakened interest was to exploit every opportunity to discredit the status quo. An article I had written for the April 1964 issue of *London Town*—the London County Council staff gazette—proved one of the most successful pieces of propaganda. It was copied both with and without my permission and subsequently appeared in journals as influential as *Local Government Finance*, the journal of the Institute of Municipal Treasurers and Accountants. The article was originally written to offer giro as the ideal solution to the problem of salary payments in an organisation as large as the London County Council—since "taken over" by the Greater London Council. Staff had recently been angered by the decision of the joint stock bank, through which their salaries were paid, to charge them for services rendered unless they maintained a minimum amount in their current accounts. In May 1964 *The Financial Times* accepted for publication the first of my letters designed to emphasise Britain's incongruous financial and economic methods in an increasingly computer-controlled civilisation supposedly modern and progressive, and extrovertly claiming its competitive abilities with the rest of the world. I shall everlastingly be grateful to the editor and staff of *The Financial Times*. They comprised the first really influential group which consistently gave me support; by the time of victory in Parliament they had published six of my letters occupying over 3 feet of column length, and continued this support so that, by the end of 1966, some twelve letters, totalling over 8 feet of column, had been published.

I wish the same could be said of the "progressive" and the "intellectual" weeklies and monthlies. On 9 July 1964 even the Fabian Society reaffirmed its decision not to publish a pamphlet devoted to giro. Discussions with officials of various organisations, professional groups in both the economic and technological fields, and firms that would directly benefit from the establishment of a British giro, showed that they were often the least co-operative. Of all the examining bodies connected with commerce, accountancy, marketing, advertising, export promotion, business administration, and systems organisation, etc., only one was progressive enough to consider introducing into its student syllabus the requirement that students must have at least some acquaintance with giro methods in continental Europe. To others the subject was "too theoretical", "too academic", "too technical", "unconnected with Commonwealth trade", "to much concerned with foreign ideas", etc. Even language text books for the teaching of French, German, etc., shunned mention of how Mr. and Mrs. Blanc, Mr. and Mrs. Schmidt, etc., were likely to pay their household bills through their local Post Office, and language teachers' organisations were completely uninterested in the omission.

One started to wonder how many years of intensive crash courses would be needed to condition the British mind sufficiently well to make it key in comfortably with the everyday customs of the European Free Trade Association or the European Economic Community.

Surprisingly enough, in view of what appeared to be the above middle-age average of many members and the banking interests represented, the rotary clubs not only gave me the best hearing but also the most sympathetic treatment.

In view of the expected appointment of Mr. James Callaghan, M.P., to a leading position concerned with finance if the Labour Party won the general election, a sentence in a letter he wrote to me on 15 April 1964 seemed a good omen indeed: "I am in favour of extending the giro system to this country."

But disappointment came a month later, when Mr. Roy Mason, M.P., wrote to suggest giro had a low priority rating. Among other Members of Parliament, the Right Hon. Douglas Houghton, M.P., emerged as a stalwart champion of legislation for a giro. Among the Parliamentary Liberal Party, Jeremy Thorpe, M.P., took a strong line in pressing for this innovation.

When I had corrected the last page-proofs of *Giro Credit Transfer Systems* and was leaving for the 1964 summer holidays, the question of a foreword for the book was still undecided. But when I returned 6 weeks later and not only found a blue-bound volume was awaiting me, but that the foreword had been contributed by no less an expert on financial and economic affairs than the Right Hon. Douglas Jay, P.C., M.P., it seemed that the struggle for a British giro service was very much more than half won. Less than a week later the leader writer of *The Financial Times*, "Lombard", wrote in his column:

"The need for the U.K. to modernise its money transmission services by introducing a postal giro system of the type operating in so many other advanced countries remains as great as

ever. If they want to know how they should set about this, the
U.K. authorities could not do better than consult the book by
Mr. F. P. Thomson on *Giro Credit Transfer Systems*."

On the same day as the above was published—3 October 1964
—Mr. Douglas Jay gave an undertaking to the National Federation of Sub-Postmasters that proposals for a British giro would
be "sympathetically examined" by a future Labour Government.

The general election came and the Labour Party was in power.
Mr. Anthony Wedgwood Benn was appointed Postmaster-
General and almost immediately set up in his department an
investigation which included visits to Europe's principal giro
countries. Much later on I was surprised to hear that for the first
time the investigators had included Sweden and Switzerland. The
omission of these countries by earlier GPO officials suggests that
the Conservatives' rejection of giro legislation in 1929 and 1963
was based on very incomplete information. And whilst this reappraisal progressed all the Giro dissidents in the country seemed
to be massing to sabotage any favourable report. A group of
young bankers brazenly asked me to help them to establish a
manually operated Giro-like system using reply-paid envelopes
for collection of customers' cheques; although the fee offered me
was attractive I gave them the same reply as I gave their successors
in a letter printed by *The Financial Times* on 21 August 1965:

"It seems appropriate to sound a warning note against the
hotheaded campaigners who think they see an opportunity to
nip in with an emergency version of the banks' own 'blueprint
for a giro' before the Post Office has time to engineer their giro
service."

The chartered accountant fraternity was angry because stream-
lined mechanization of business systems using computer compatible documents provided by a Giro centre might reduce the
lucrative examination of paperwork on which many younger
accountants flourished; the anonymous commentator of *The
Accountant* in writing a review of my first book sailed pretty close

to a defamatory description of me when reviewing it. But I soon grew accustomed to being on the receiving end of personal abuse and worse; after two physical attacks and threats against my wife's safety I began to wonder what would come next. Most surprisingly, it was aggressive opposition by trade unionists and some members of the Labour Party who saw Giro as a threat to that most sacred of Labour movement ideals, the Co-operative Wholesale Society Bank. As it was perfectly obvious that left-wing socialists were urging renationalisation of steel as a first priority in the hope of taking the heat off pressures for Giro legislation, I mounted a counter-propaganda operation. The last paragraph of a letter from me in *The Financial Times* of February 17, 1965, warned:

> "If the British Government wants to lay the foundation for the scientifically administered society which the General Election speeches promised us, and at the same time wishes to make itself rapidly popular in every business and home in the country (with the possible exception of a few of the bankers), it will legislate for a Post Office Giro before the renationalisation of steel."

Although trade unionists angrily dubbed me a "traitor of the working-class" and assured me that "no Labour Government would dare upset the chances of a bank with such admirable ideals as the Co-op. Bank", and even some Post Office employees endeavoured to make me disgorge the original copies of letters I had received from pro-giro parliamentarians because they felt giro promotion ought to have been progressed exclusively by Post Office people, there were—fortunately—a number of indications (including the ferocity of anti-giroists) that the reappraisal was proving favourable. In an effort to silence the noisy and annoying anti-giro trade unionists I wrote to the CWS Bank and suggested their service might be enhanced if they established a bank giro to operate through the nation-wide chain of Co-op. retail shops open throughout normal business hours. They replied on 13 May 1965:

". . . after full consideration I would say that so far as the
Bank is concerned the facilities already provided for our
customers to transfer funds from their accounts as required,
are regarded as ample and easy of operation. Moreover these
facilities are available at a minimum of cost to the customer."

As it is typical of the sort of self-satisfied propaganda that was
thrown at me by Labour movement anti-giro aggressives, and
appeared as if by coincidence after contributions of mine on the
National Giro in the October and December 1966 issues of
Plebs the following extracts from an article in the January 1967
issue (reprinted from the *South Kensington Labour Report*) are
included to indicate that it is not only the bankers and banking
public of the right who could menace the popularity of a post
office Giro:

". . . Though of course the Co-op. carries on huge trade
union and other Labour movement business, it welcomes the
small fry too. But for practical purposes of paying the gas and
electricity and the rent bill and bills at the Co-op. it is more
than adequate for the normal wage and salary earner. . . . You
can cash your cheques at the local Co-op. shops. . . . And I
don't have shares—only in the sense that we all have a share
and an interest in the Co-op. movement."

Continuing rumours that legislation was almost out of sight at
the bottom of a long list of priorities was indeed depressing. The
hard-won but mounting enthusiasm infecting an increasing number of people from about 1963 threatened to dwindle unless there
was positive proof of action soon. Fresh approaches to the broad-
casting and television authorities with the suggestion of mounting
a feature on "This Thing Called Giro" or "Not Gyro But Giro"
were either rejected or did not receive even an acknowledgement.
The new Government had a minute majority and I felt we might
be working against time both as regards the strains on greatly
fatigued Members of Parliament and the clamour for early
renationalisation of the steel industry—a measure so controversial

that it might bring the Government down. Moreover, I very strongly felt the Government ought to face early on the essentiality of establishing a giro as the only reasonable national foundation for business efficiency generation and computer technology progress. And so, instead of returning to my professional work in a very different sphere, after *Giro Credit Transfer Systems* was published I continued the British Giro Campaign. Moreover, I received more requests to write articles and to address groups than could have been accommodated otherwise. To be in demand at last, instead of a seeker of ways to promote information about giro, was a well worthwhile change, and came not a moment too soon after years of frustration.

The long-awaited sign that the time had come for legislation was contained in a letter written on 7 July 1965 by the Prime Minister, the Right Hon. Harold Wilson, P.C., M.P. (Fig. 36), from 10 Downing Street, Whitehall:

DEAR MR. THOMSON,

"Thank you for sending me the recent issue of 'Credit' containing your article on the Giro.

"As you will know, the possibility of introducing a Post Office Giro is being studied now and there is to be a short debate on a Private Member's Motion later this month.

"I am familiar with your previous work in this field and I am glad to see that you are once again raising the matter for public discussion.

Yours sincerely,
(signed) HAROLD WILSON."

4.5. Victory in Parliament

On Wednesday afternoon, 21 July 1965, I was shown to a seat in the Public Gallery of the House of Commons, just before 4 o'clock.

A few minutes later the Member for Accrington, Mr. Harry

Fig. 36. The Prime Minister, the Right Hon. Harold Wilson, P.C., M.P.

Hynd, rose to move the motion: "That this House would welcome the establishment of a postal giro service in the United Kingdom offering similar facilities to those given by postal giro systems in other countries."

During the ensuing debate, lasting barely 180 minutes, the merits and demerits of giro as seen by Labour, Conservative, and Liberal speakers were thoroughly but amicably discussed, and when the question was put, would the House agree to the motion, the Opposition did not press for a division.

With the intoning by the Speaker of the age-old phrase indicating that another motion had been accepted by Parliament, "The ayes have it, the ayes have it", I suddenly realised that I had not only witnessed a reform that in the years to come will have an increasingly great and beneficial effect on the lives of all of us, but that I had, in some ways, been almost as much involved as the Members on the floor of the House. Few authors of first books see their volume in the hands of Members of Parliament and hear it referred to during a debate resulting in a national reform. It was an experience of which dreams are made.

Following this historic event, a proposal was made that a sequel to *Giro Credit Transfer Systems* should be written and that this new book should not only be a record that would spur others to press for a similar reform in their country, but would also assist students and the general reader in Britain and elsewhere to recognise the relationship between money management, computer technology, and business system efficiency. In response to an invitation to the principal participants in this reform to outline their views on its significance, the following contributions were received.

THE POSTMASTER-GENERAL, then ANTHONY WEDGWOOD BENN, P.C., M.P. (Fig. 37), asked that selected quotations be printed from his speech during the debate.

"One of the first things I did on taking office was to commission a fresh study of the giro as a possibility. This has been done with very great thoroughness. Further visits were made

FIG. 37. The Postmaster-General was Mr. Anthony Wedgwood Benn at the time Parliament agreed to the motion authorising the establishment of a British Post Office giro service.

to Europe to study the latest experience there. Up-to-date
surveys were made of the need and prospects. The review
revealed certain new factors which led us to consider the
matter in a more favourable light than the last Government
had done.

"The first thing which came to light was the growing need
for certain sorts of service not provided by the present remittance services of the Post Office or the money transmission
facilities in this country. For example, over the last seven years,
the mail order business has doubled in size. This is a clear
indication of the need for some means by which remittances on
this scale can be made available. Secondly, instalment payments,
which are very important, have doubled in the last four years.
Both these things are likely to increase still further. Turning to
credit shopping, there is the renting of durable consumer goods,
like television sets.

"All these are things that have developed very greatly in
this country. At the moment, people deal with them very often
by cash payments in local offices or by postal orders or money
orders, which are very old-fashioned and extremely expensive
ways of transmitting money. This is done by people who do
not have bank accounts. It is not a question whether a bank can
offer its customers improved facilities, although that is something which naturally everybody welcomes. The question is
what should be done about people who do not have joint stock
bank current accounts. At any rate, as a result of our survey of
the need, we came to the conclusion that the financial prospects
for a giro were very much improved.

"The question of market research has, very properly, been
raised. What the Post Office is considering is this: can we
modernise our existing remittance services? If so, in what way
should we modernise them? If we modernise them in a certain
way, what price would we have to charge and what is the
potential demand?

"I can only tell the House that on our basis of calculation
at the moment it would be possible not just to break even, but

to get an 8 per cent return over the long run on a giro system with as few as $1\frac{1}{4}$ million giro account holders with an average balance of only between £100 and £150. All I can say about that is that if we compare those very cautious assumptions with the experience on the Continent we shall realise that assumptions of this kind really are more than reasonable.

". . . As a result of this survey the Government have decided that a Post Office giro, offering the same basic facilities as the European giro, would be a useful addition to the means of transmitting money, to the normal Post Office remittance services, which have been more or less unchanged since 1881, and it would provide a cheap and efficient service for those without normal banking facilities who do not want the full range of services offered by joint stock banks.

". . . I come to the next question, which is, relations with the joint stock banks. I am very grateful that this point has been raised because it is, of course, very important indeed. We believe that the giro will be popular with those without bank accounts, of whom there are very large numbers, of course— an overall majority in this country. Hence the giro will, in terms of the individual, be moving into a more or less untapped market from the banks' point of view, and it will be replacing in this respect the existing Post Office remittance services.

"This is the point I made earlier in respect of market research and a point made by the hon. Gentleman the Member for Moray and Nairn. We contemplate this as a modernisation of our own remittance services, and it follows from this that we see the giro as complementing the banking services and not replacing them. Having said that, it is quite clear that there must be links between the giro and the banks from the point of view of the national interest. If the nation is to have a comprehensive, modern, money transmission system, there must be quick and easy transfers between giro accounts and ordinary bank accounts.

". . . To sum up, I would say that the Government are convinced that they would be offering cheap and speedy

FIG. 38. Mr. Harry Hynd, J.P., M.P., moved the motion in favour of
establishing a British giro.

facilities to meet a real need not met by existing facilities. It is on this basis that we make this announcement to the House.

". . . This is a great step forward. It is a notable addition to Post Office services and to public enterprise which I should like to see meet the needs of the community. If it can do so it will boost computer technology in this country, and will lead to a demand for more computers. It will meet the sophisticated needs of a modern society.

". . . I hope, therefore, that the House will endorse the Motion, so ably moved by my hon. Friend the Member for Accrington, and give us the go-ahead to get on with the job."

(The above was extracted from *Hansard: House of Commons Debates*, 21 July 1965, v. 716, no. 158, cols. 1633–42.)

HARRY HYND, J.P., then MEMBER OF PARLIAMENT FOR ACCRINGTON (Fig. 38):

"Since Mr. Wedgwood Benn made his historic announcement in the House of Commons on 21st July 1965 that the British Post Office would introduce a Giro system there has been a demand for information on this subject.

"Those who need specialised information have ample resources, but it is for the less technically minded that Mr. Thomson has written this popular shorter version of his main book *Giro Credit Transfer Systems*.

"After all, it is the man in the street who will benefit most from Giro, whether as a cheap and easy way to pay his accounts, his rent and his hire purchase instalments; as a safer and more convenient way of getting his wages; or as a practical and attractive method of saving. This book explains in simple terms just how the scheme will work.

"It is worth stressing that Giro has been operated successfully in many countries over a long period, so it is not an untried idea. It will be a boon to those who, for whatever reason, do not require the full-scale services of a bank cheque book."

FIG. 39. Mr. Jeremy Thorpe, M.P., for long a prominent Liberal Party
spokesman in favour of establishing a British giro service, was elected the
Leader of his Party in the House of Commons in January 1967.

JEREMY THORPE, MEMBER OF PARLIAMENT FOR DEVON NORTH (Fig. 39), asked that his speech during the debate should be paraphrased, but perhaps the simplest way would be to quote those parts which touch on aspects of giro not emphasised by other speakers:

"I intervene in the debate briefly to give my warm support to the Motion. Not for the first time have I supported a Motion of this kind and I hope that at last action will be taken on the subject.

". . . Crime has been mentioned. I agree with the hon. Member for Watford that the Payment of Wages Act has not produced the fall in payment by cash that one would have hoped for, and this system is one means by which it could be brought about. It would also save a fair amount of duplication and, as a result, a fair amount of labour.

"The giro system would be particularly valuable in the rural areas. Many rural people have cars, but those who do not are finding that communications are becoming increasingly difficult. Many branch railway lines have been closed down, and a good many bus services are being restricted. It is becoming steadily more difficult in remote rural areas for people to get to the electricity or gas offices to pay their bills. They would be immediately benefited by the giro system. I do not know whether, statutorily, nationalised industries are directed or persuaded but, in any event, such nationalised industries as gas and electricity should be encouraged to open giro accounts. Similarly, the system could be used for the payment of rates, and many other payments in respect of public services could be channelled through the Post Office system. Competition with our existing banks would also be a very good thing to have. There is nothing like competition; no human organisation exists that does not benefit by it.

". . . I urge this on the right hon. Gentleman, not because it is Socialism or Liberalism, but because it will be good business for the Post Office, and a very real convenience to the public at large."

Fig. 40. Mr. Harry E. Randall, M.P., a former Post Office worker, took a leading part in the debate in favour of the motion.

(The aforementioned was extracted from *Hansard: House of Commons Debates*, v. 716, no. 158, cols. 1609–13.)

HARRY E. RANDALL, MEMBER OF PARLIAMENT FOR GATESHEAD WEST (Fig. 40):

"A simple and straightforward system of transferring credits of both large and small amounts to meet the demands of business and domestic life is urgently required and would be of real benefit to all.

"There are, in this country, a large number of people who do not need or require the more elaborate and expensive system provided by the joint stock banks. What they do require, instead of handing round the loose change of pennies and half-pennies, silver, 10/– and £1 notes; the expensive and cumbersome purchase of postal orders and money orders; the savings in the jar on the mantelpiece and the sock under the bed, in order to meet their regular payments and accounts, is a simple and secure service which eliminates risks, reduces costs and is on their doorstep.

"The Giro service operated by the Post Office with its 23 000 offices scattered over the length and breadth of the land, offers this greatest step forward to a community whose members are increasingly in need of such a service."

RAPHAEL TUCK, MEMBER OF PARLIAMENT FOR WATFORD (Fig. 41):

"Giro means to me the end of outdated, costly, cumbersome, lengthy, inefficient and almost Heath-Robinsonian methods of money transmission, and the introduction of a modern, cost-free, simple, speedy, efficient and stream-lined system of banking and credit transfer. It means the substitution of the computer for the match-sticks, and giving to the masses of the

FIG. 41. Mr. Raphael Tuck, M.P. (right), contributed forcibly to the debate on the motion in favour of establishing a British giro, and is seen here with the Author at the press reception following Parliament's agreement to the introduction of this important reform.

Fig. 41

people the opportunity of having credit facilities, while denying to the criminal the opportunity of violent physical attacks on members of the public and banking staffs.

"Finally, it means immense potential advantages to the British financial, economic and social structure, and great potential strides in the progress of British trade abroad. The Giro system has long been overdue in Britain. There is no excuse for any delay further in its introduction."

Two of the principal speakers for the Opposition were the Right Hon. Ray Mawby, Member of Parliament for Totnes (Fig. 42), and Gordon T. C. Campbell, M.C., Member of Parliament for Moray and Nairn (Fig. 43). Both had considerable previous experience of the giro question and made significant contributions to the debate. The following quotations are from *Hansard: House of Commons Debates*, v. 716, no. 158, and the column number precedes the quotation.

THE RIGHT HON. RAY MAWBY, MEMBER OF PARLIAMENT FOR TOTNES (cols. 1594–1602):

"Upon first coming into office and upon hearing the case so well put by the late Will Williams, I was attracted to the scheme. It has attractions. After all, it makes it possible to make certain that wages can be paid by cheque, or, indeed, as the hon. Gentleman has said, to be paid directly into one's account by quoting one's number. Obviously there would be far less cash moving about the country because it would be a matter of credit being transferred from one person to another, and so there would be less opportunity for the many robberies which take place, and which, we must always remember, while involving property, also involve so many postmen and others who are thus brought into danger—of being coshed for instance —and of suffering very badly indeed.

"At first sight the scheme is very attractive indeed. There is also the other point the hon. Gentleman put, that the post offices normally are open for longer hours than the joint stock

FIG. 42. The Right Hon. Ray Mawby, the Opposition's spokesman in Parliament on 21 July 1965.

banks. To the ordinary person wanting to transact business the fact that the post offices are open very often at times when he ceases, or before he begins, work gives it an additional attraction.

"However, I think that, after one has said that, one has to look very closely at the whole system and particularly where it has been in operation for many years, as the hon. Gentleman has said, in various Continental countries.

". . . One of the great advantages of this system is that it enables an undertaking to reduce the number of its employees. For example, in the normal course of events an electricity undertaking ensures that a cashier is on duty in its showroom. It is his job to accept money from people paying bills, to give them receipts and change. If, however, that undertaking had a giro account, all the people to whom it sent bills could transact their business at the post office rather than go to the showroom, and it has been shown that people would rather carry out the physical side of a business transaction in places other than electricity showrooms and insurance offices.

". . . We would have one advantage, that we could install the most modern equipment from scratch, learning from the experience of those on the Continent who are only now, in certain places, installing computers and memory-stores. However, even with that advantage, the capital cost of a system such as this would be very heavy. . . . The Postmaster General has far more up-to-date facts and figures than I, but I felt I ought to put my views to the House, as one who was attracted on first sight to the system and who, even now, is not prepared to condemn it. I have tried to put some of the problems we will have to face, inevitably, if the scheme is introduced."

GORDON T. C. CAMPBELL, M.C., MEMBER OF PARLIAMENT FOR MORAY AND NAIRN (cols. 1618–22):

"My reason for taking part in this debate is that I have lived in a country with a giro system. When I was a diplomatist in Europe, I lived in the country which we have been told by the

FIG. 43. Mr. Gordon T. C. Campbell, M.C., M.P., was probably the only Member of Parliament with personal experience of continental giro system operation. He was also one of Parliament's experts on decimal currency and a strong advocate of a 10s. unit.

hon. Member for Accrington was the founder of the system, namely, Austria. I have made many payments by the giro system. I also took the opportunity of studying it and examining it, simply as a matter of interest, its suitability and adaptability for this country.

"... This system is needed by the countries in Europe and it is useful there, but they have very different banking and other conditions. For historical reasons, our situation is not the same as that in those countries which have the giro system.

"If sufficient support were forthcoming for the system, I would be in favour at first sight of its adoption. There is an alternative which has not been mentioned so far, namely, a combination with the banking system. . . .

"Several hon. Members have mentioned the crime aspect. As the system would largely obviate sending money by post, it would remove the motive of many of the crimes concerning mail bags and against postmen.

"... If most wage earners were prepared to use the system, that would probably have the effect of encouraging savings, as the hon. Member for Gateshead West said, and the scheme would then have so much support that it would probably be efficient and worth putting into effect. We understand that the banks are now threatening that they may not open on Saturday mornings, and that would deprive many people of the opportunity of making payments at a time when post offices were open. . . .

"As the House will realise, having seen and lived with this system, I am attracted by it, but, in my view, it is important that we do not enter upon it here until we are certain that it will have the right measure of support. . . ."

With reference to the suggestion made by Mr. Campbell that a giro should be worked in combination with the banking system, it is noteworthy that the (then) Postmaster-General included this in his speech (*Hansard: House of Commons Debates*, v. 716, no. 158, col. 1639):

". . . If the nation is to have a comprehensive, modern, money transmission system, there must be quick and easy transfers between giro accounts, and I am confident that satisfactory arrangements with the banks will be reached for direct transfers between bank accounts and giro accounts, and *vice versa*.

"I very much hope that we shall also be able to reach agreement on another important point, namely, the compatibility in design of bank and giro forms, because what we are concerned with here is a national system which meets the requirements of a wide variety of people."

CHAPTER 5

Monetary Methods for a Technocracy

By NOW the reader will have realised that a giro has many facets, and will have drawn his own conclusions as to why legislation for this reform was so long hindered.

A survey of literature shows that not until about 1964 was giro recognised as one of the principal keys to unlocking computer applications on a national scale, and therefore of massive importance in planning a strategy of scientifically based national economy. As the recognition of giro in this context came so much later than in neighbouring European countries, British management systems will have to undergo phenomenally rapid changes if administrative techniques are to be aligned on a competitive basis with the neat and efficient monetary and marketing methods for so long enjoyed by Swedish and West German, French and Dutch, and other European commercial enterprises and institutions. The organisation of monetary movement—in exchange for goods and services—is one of the most common exercises in nearly every office and so the substitution of Britain's archaic and cumbersome methods for giro methods should prove a good tonic and discipline, and encourage management to seek out more efficient ways of accomplishing other workaday office tasks. One can often produce great savings in manpower and materials by analysing office routines with the help of a flow diagram like those in this book.

The establishment of the National Giro and then decimal currency in a period of only 3 years will shake to the core a wide range of British customs and institutions. To many people, nothing is quite so sacrosanct as money. When two reforms like these uproot all previous habits one might expect chaos if not open rebellion. But, viewed dispassionately, it would be wise to remember that we are only catching up, in a single 3-year leap, on what most of western Europe has been doing for years past.

We will even benefit from the experience of computer-centred automated giro systems pioneered, for example, by Austria, whose computer-controlled Giro Centre went into operation in 1962, and Sweden's advanced automated Giro Centre—which introduced optically read electronically actuated cheque handling equipment in 1966. In the same year—1959—as the report of the Committee on the Working of the Monetary System was published, commending the establishment of a British Post Office giro, the Netherlands Post Office issued its report on machine-read document experiments. Its own computer-centred and automated giro centre went into operation in 1962. In fact nearly all of Europe's giro authorities had either issued proposals for the conversion of their systems to computer control or were operating such a system when Britain's Parliament was merely deciding whether to support the motion in favour of establishing a giro.

Considerable mirth was caused in continental giro centres when the British journal, *Socialist Commentary*, published an article by Charles Morris, M.P., in its March 1967 issue under the title, "The British Giro". The paragraphs which caused amusement—and some annoyance—were:

"It may well be the case that the British Giro will not be patterned exactly on any of the Continental systems. I should hope it will not. To my knowledge, these are all old-fashioned services, basically the same but differing from one another in method of operation and facilities. And so it should be with the British system. Indeed, I will be most disappointed if the Post Office does not offer us a model Giro system. With so much experience available to draw on, the British service should be an amalgam of all that is best elsewhere.

"This, I think, will prove to be the case. The British system appears potentially more flexible than any single existing system. It will be computer-based from the start and the most advanced installation of its kind in the world. In these respects at least it will be the envy of every other Giro which has had, or is facing, the formidable task of converting its manual or semi-automatic system to computer working. If this is what deviation from the traditional Giro pattern means, then I am all for it. And all praise to the Post Office for turning its back on tradition and striking out boldly in this way."

The most common west European comment was: "whilst our 'old-fashioned services' appear to be adequately meeting the needs of our country's trade, the British (as usual) are boasting with nothing to show for it!"

5.1.   Giro's First Impact on British Computer Progress

Just over a year after the Postmaster-General (then Mr. Anthony Wedgwood Benn), prophesied in the House of Commons that a giro ". . . will boost computer technology in this country, and will lead to a demand for more computers," the English Electric Leo Marconi Company announced in *The Financial Times* of 1 August 1966 (Fig. 44): "We've just won the biggest computer contract ever, outside the U.S.A."

This was for £3 million worth of large System 4–70 machines, of which two were part of the initial equipment for the National Giro Centre, destined to be eventually one of the largest computer complexes in Europe, two were for the Post Office Savings Bank installation at Glasgow, and one for a Post Office regional centre. The contract included the supply of a complete set of programmes for the Giro Centre, and the option to purchase a further four similar machines at a price of some £2 million.

FIG. 44. This full-page advertisement in *The Financial Times* of Monday, 1 August 1966, proved that the long campaign for a British giro service had, at last, unlocked both a vast market for British computers and the greater utilisation of these efficiency-promoting, electronically controlled devices.

Fig. 44

On 1 February 1967 the British Olivetti Company announced it had been awarded a contract to supply the Giro Centre with £250 000 worth of transcribing encoders to process handwritten data into machine readable form.

And on 7 March 1967 the Recognition Equipment Company announced it was to supply over £900 000 worth of its Electronic Retina optical read-out equipment. This wonderful invention was first installed in a Giro Centre in 1965–6, and Fig. 45 shows the computer hall of Sweden's Post Giro Centre where the Electronic Retina is now making light work—in both meanings—of the daily massive load of giro form encoding. The Electronic Retina is typical of the sort of complex invention the special requirements of banking automation has stimulated, and is a good example of how electro-mechanical devices can eliminate humdrum chores formerly performed by clerks.

This device (Fig. 46) is similar to the reader's eye in its ability to discriminate the significant features comprising information to be transmitted from a giro form, even if the writing is smudged and confused by trivial scrawls; it tolerates and makes allowances for variations in ink density, accidental breaks in the written line, variations in line pitch, page position, and character pattern differences.

A contract to supply data input equipment was awarded to the Standard Telephones and Cables Company.

To meet the scheduled opening date for the National Giro it proved necessary to incorporate foreign designed equipment, but it must be noted with due respect that much of the initial development of the type of character-recognition systems the Giro Centre will use was originated about 1956–7 by British Electronic Engineers working at the National Physical Laboratory at Teddington, Middlesex. As has so often happened, the ideas of British engineers were exploited abroad, and then called into British service in foreign-designed equipment.

FIG. 45. This view of one of the Stockholm Giro Centre's computer halls is the twentieth-century equivalent of the nineteenth century's myriad of pen-pushing clerks perched on three-legged stools filling columns in heavy ledgers.

FIG. 45

And so, well before the actual opening of the National Giro, and as an ominous indication of how deeply parliamentary equivocation up to 1965 had impeded the application of technology for the national benefit, we were beginning to experience the effect of the "great step forward" Mr. Anthony Wedgwood Benn as Postmaster-General had foreseen when he supported the giro motion. This, indeed, was a great improvement from the gloomy prospects of barely 2 years previously, when the United Kingdom used more imported than domestically made computers. *The Financial Times* reported, on 4 April 1965: "Deliveries of imported computers in the U.K. last year outpaced those of British-built machines for the third year running."

5.1.1. THE COST OF ESTABLISHING THE NATIONAL GIRO

During the historic debate on the motion the Postmaster-General estimated the capital cost of installing equipment for the National Giro Centre would be £4 to £5 million spread over 5 to 6 years, and operating costs would be some £15 million per annum. This estimate was based on an initial 1.25 million account holders with an average balance of £100 to £150 each. He claimed it would not only be possible to break even but to get an 8 per cent return over the long run, and operating costs would be jointly financed by the interest earned on money held in transit and by charges, e.g. for services between non-giroists and giroists.

The subsequent public interest in the National Giro suggests that the estimate of only 1.25 million account holders was too low for the first few years, and that this may be exceeded by 100 per cent. But if 1.25 million was a viable figure to make the service profitable from inauguration, then this should encourage many other countries to install the same highly automated equipment and to launch giros too.

Even if Britain's total population were to produce only 1.25 million giroists, the percentage would be the same as that of Norway and Austria. In 1965, by contrast, Belgium had 10.6 per cent of its population as giroists; Holland had 9.0 per cent;

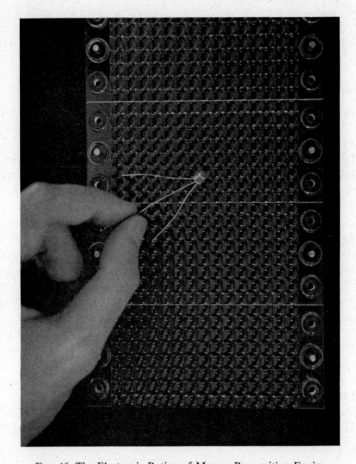

FIG. 46. The Electronic Retina of Messrs. Recognition Equipment's automatic form-reading equipment for the National Giro Centre is typical of the ingenious technical devices which technologists will be called upon to invent as the banking applications for computer-actuated networks advance still further. This photograph shows a small section of the human-eye-like retina.

Morocco had 6.0 per cent; Luxembourg had 10.7 per cent; and France had 12.7 per cent. About as much money was transferred through post offices from non-giroists to giroists as between giroists.

The cost of establishing Britain's giro is astonishingly small even if the cost of the Giro Centre building at Bootle—some £2 million—and the £1 million allocated for publicity are included.

There is always the nice question as to whether a public service of such power for good should be costed strictly on commercial lines, satisfactory though it will be if entirely profitable. To be completely honest one ought to set against the cost of establishing the National Giro the savings it creates in other sectors of the nation's affairs. For example, one ought to place to the credit of giro the reduction in insurance arising from the lowered risk of loss and theft when credit transfers are substituted for the criminally vulnerable storage and transit of cash; the reduction of expenditure on safes, money-boxes, strongrooms, armed guards to protect wages money collection; the reduced demand for police services expended in apprehending and bringing to justice the crooks who hold up bank cashiers, kill and maim sub-postmasters, waylay wages clerks, and cosh the small shopkeeper. Crime has been increasing for years, but the scientific criminal may find giro virtually impossible to crack to his advantage on a worthwhile scale. The now almost legendary Great Train Robbery, with the theft by armed bandits of some £2 million could have only happened in a pre-giro Britain and it is perhaps ironical that this event took place only a few miles from Watford during the latter stages of the British Giro Campaign.

There is also the immense saving in paperwork to be put to the credit of giro operation costs, and the saving of time in the storage and retrieval of payment documents, a saving which effects private homes as much as business concerns. Then there are the inestimable profits when the risk of bodily attack and death of people whose job it has been to collect money from banks for wage payments is abolished in favour of payment of wages by giro.

The *Post Office Report and Accounts* 1965–6, p. 56, gives Giro Development Expenses at 31 March 1966 as amounting to only £67 550, which is little enough considering the immensity of the task in setting up the framework for this innovation.

It is worth noting that when Belgium's long-established post office giro service (founded 1913) changed over to automated working the cost was greater than the total cost of establishing Britain's National Giro. According to a report in *The Financial Times* of 13 August 1965, p. 5:

"Machinery providing complete automatic handling for the first 100 000 accounts in the Belgian Post Office banking system was brought into operation to-day. The machinery was devised for the job by the Bell Telephone Company of Antwerp, a member of the International Telegraph and Telephone group.

"Complete automation of the system will be provided within two years by the installation of nine further sets of machines of similar capacity. The total cost will then have been rather over £7 million or £7 per account."

The British Postmaster-General's estimate in 1965 of £4–£5 million worth of capital equipment to open a service with an initial 1.25 million account holders, gives an average of *only* £4 per account holder for capital cost. It is understood this amount is likely to be even less because the capacity may be greater than 1.25 million account holders. This low cost for installing a new giro service ought to encourage smaller nations to follow Britain's lead.

Nor is £15 million an unreasonable operating cost compared with the Swedish Post Giro, for example—one of Europe's most successful systems. At about the same time as Mr. Anthony Wedgwood Benn's Post Office administration was carrying out its survey of the possibilities of a British giro—that is—from the latter part of 1964, the Swedish Post Giro had 0.5 million account holders and, during the financial year of 1964 cost £12.5 million to operate, which averages £25 per account holder, a seemingly high figure compared with the £12 per account holder prophecy of the (then) Postmaster-General. In the same year the Swedish Post Giro earned £608 000 surplus despite the interest rate on invested giro balances falling short of the 8 per cent anticipated by the British Postmaster-General for the National Giro. The average cost of Swedish giro transactions was about 11*d*. each; the charge for transactions between giroists was nil and no lower or upper limit on amount was set; the fee for transfers between giroists and non-giroists, or vice versa, was about 4*d*. each; transfers to giroists in other Scandinavian countries were free as within Sweden itself and transfers to giroists in other countries were charged about 5*d*., whilst outpayments to non-giroists abroad cost approximately 1*s*. each, plus airmail postage. The exchange rate used was Kr 14:50 to £1 sterling.

Attention should be drawn at this point to the immense encouragement given, through giro, to the Swedish public to think in terms of computer techniques, or to be curious about the impact on their daily lives of methods derived from this source. Figure 47 depicts a typical advertisement, one of many which daily focus attention on the effect of computers on Sweden's everyday life, and help to make every Swede aware of new concepts of business efficiency. In contrast, the British public is not alert to computer applications to anything like such a marked degree; a harmful position for one of the world's main computer producing countries!

5.2.   The Joint Stock Banks Modernise to Compete

From aggressive rumblings about a competitive giro if the Post Office dared to go ahead with the establishment of a giro, the reaction of the joint stock banks appeared to be one of relief

FIG. 47. Advertisements like this for the Swedish Post Office giro's services bring a knowledge of computer techniques into the home of every Swede and also a realisation of the benefits conferred by processing business and private payments by giro methods. Following the establishment of the National Giro's services it is to be expected that a similar awareness will activate public thinking in Britain to the great advantage of both the national economy and technology.

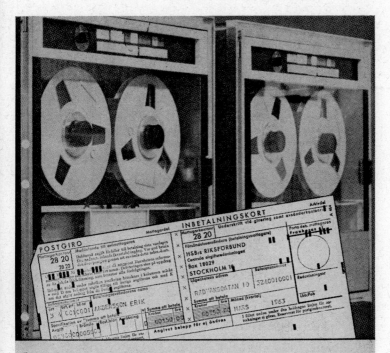

Fig. 47

when the Government white paper, *A Post Office Giro*, was published in August 1965.

Quite a few bankers privately held the view expressed by one of them to the author:

"The giro will at last relieve us from having to provide what amounts to a completely unprofitable public service, which has been the cross we bear for enjoying a monopoly in commercial banking. We dare not charge an economic amount for the myriad of very small accounts many small trades people, pensioners and poorer people keep with us, for fear of frightening off their sons and daughters whose rising salary scales make them potentially worth while clients. We feel it is our duty to give the pensioner the same standard of service as we accorded him as a businessman and he, as an old client and friend, expects the same relationship to continue. But banking is an increasingly costly business and equipment and labour costs are taking their toll and so we, too, have to study profit margins very critically."

Retirement pensioners will increase nationally until about 1980, when the number will even out to about 8.25 million persons in 1990, an increase of nearly 40 per cent in 30 years. A giro has obvious advantages for them.

But there was something near an explosion in banking circles when the booklet, *The National Giro—The New Current Account Banking Service*, was published in July–August 1966. Bankers took the view that the plans proposed: ". . . did not bear out statements in the White Paper and by the Postmaster-General that the new Giro service was to be complementary to the existing banking service."

Reaction was rapid. On 2 March 1967 the Banking Information Service issued an announcement that the London clearing banks and the Scottish banks would inaugurate new services including:

1. A bank customers' direct debiting service, with optional facilities for magnetic tape information exchange between banks and computer-using customers.

2. A free credit transfer service for customers, with no limit on maximum and minimum amounts. Non-customers would be charged 6*d*. per transfer, or 1*s*. if made direct from bank to bank.
3. The replacement of the periodic bank statement by a system of rapid advice notes, when delay in rendering returns to larger users would be inconvenient.
4. A salary, wage, and pension expedited payment system for employers issuing 1000 or more credits simultaneously.
5. Improved design of credit transfer forms with the addition of a message space.

Whether or not the plans published in *The National Giro—The New Current Account Banking Service* as "the main facilities to be provided at the outset" conflicted, as bankers claim, is debatable, but there followed very soon a positive indication of how much the banks' former monopolistic hold on commercial account banking had halted the introduction of modern technological method, and how deeply the establishment of the National Giro had stirred apathy.

During April 1967 the banks placed orders for over £20 million worth of computers and ancillaries to improve counter services and to make their customer-appeal comparable with that of the National Giro. By the beginning of November 1967 the figure had risen to a committed £100 million worth or more of computers to match the Post Office counter and giro bank facilities. These installations will be among the largest in Europe and bring Britain to the threshold of a prophecy made by Mr. Dale L. Reistad, Director of Automation and Marketing Research, American Bankers Association (*Banking Journal of the American Bankers Association*, July 1964):

"In estimated data transmission investment, banking already ranks fourth among all industries (see table below). By 1975 it is possible that banking, because of the many new data transmission applications still in their infancy, may be the single largest user of machine-to-machine communications.

"The entire banking industry would benefit greatly if marketing research statistics, by area, were collected regularly at a central point, and made available to all subscribing banks for use both in selling bank services and in assisting a bank's business customers. (Where in N.W. United States would consumer demand be greatest for laminated wallboard? How many general practitioners among doctors are there in the Rocky Mountain states and what percentage buy medical supplies through out-of-state drug warehouses?) Such a plan is feasible today. It will be desirable tomorrow and may become an accepted way of doing banking in 1975.

"With expanding world-wide business broadening the market for financial service, is it not reasonable to believe that by 1975 banks will be engaged in machine-to-machine communications on behalf of their customers to banks in Italy, Thailand and Iran; and conducting transactions across continents with as much ease as today banks transmit general ledger information from a branch to the central office?

"By 1970 banks will probably be offering "Dial-In" services to small businesses and even regular customers whereby a customer can pay a bill by simply pulling the proper plastic card out of a file (the Gas and Electric Company), and inserting it in the telephone (the card contains the bank's "Dial-In" number, the customer number and the Gas and Electric number) and keying in the amount of the bill (depressing 2, 5, 0, 0 for $25.00). The transactions will be completed by the bank either in real-time or off-time processing on the bank's general purpose computer system.

"Banking automation by 1975 will have a profound effect on the people as well as the operations. New needs will create new jobs in research, service development, computer programming, system and procedures, communications, statistics, merchandising, sales, forward planning, operations research, and human factors research.

1965 Computer rental values in millions of dollars, by industries:

Large electronics and aerospace manufacturers:	10.3
Primary metal manufacturers:	9.7
State and local government:	8.5
Banks:	6.8
Utilities:	6.7
Insurance companies:	4.6
Petrochemical manufacturers:	4.1
Transportation:	4.1
Financial and brokerage houses:	3.7
Automobile manufacturers:	2.3
Department stores and large retail firms:	2.9
Data processing service bureaux:	1.8
Newspaper publishing firms:	1.5"

5.3. A Model for American Banking to Copy?

Despite the large number of immigrants from European giro countries who have discussed with fellow Americans the advantages of the system, the idea does not appear to have taken root and this is probably because of the absence of a central source of comprehensive information in the English language, or exactly the same problem which prompted the writing of *Giro Credit Transfer Systems*.

The Report of the Committee on the Working of the Monetary System states, in paragraph 958, p. 330:

"In the United States of America the demand for a simple chequing service has to some extent been met by the banking system; many banks have established a personal cheque service. One of the 'big five' banks in the United Kingdom introduced a similar service in September 1958, 'designed to meet the demands of people requiring a standard, limited banking service, provided at the lowest possible cost, known in advance'. This bank has reported that 'large numbers of personal cheque accounts are being opened every day ... and the average balance in such accounts has exceeded our expectations'."

But by 1964 Britain's annual turnover of cheques had reached such a huge volume that thoughts were being turned to the establishment of a single, centralised clearing organisation for all the clearing banks, like that operated from a country centre during the 1939–45 war. Instead, the joint stock banks continued to work largely independently which, of course, increased the total cost of automated cheque clearing. In June 1967, therefore, the national system was strained under an operational load of processing 299 005 million articles, representing a 4.7 per cent rise since June 1966. In the same period there had been a rise in value in cheques cleared of some 20.6 per cent.

The British joint stock banks' cheque clearance problems were not without parallel in the United States of America where a mere 76 000 million cheques per annum, according to the reported speech of Mr. Herbert J. Blitz—a research director of the Diebold Europa organisation—was creating a serious blockage. The seminar attended by Mr. Blitz was held in London in June 1966 and excited considerable speculation regarding the future of banking in the computer age. In the same speech Mr. Blitz is reported as having commented on the adverse effects of weather, geography, and distances on American banking when compared with British conditions, and that the handling of cheques in the U.S.A. represents some 60 per cent of the cost of their banking services. He visualised the development of a combined credit and identity card which, at the time of making a purchase, could be keyed into a vast, complex, and nationwide computer-controlled accountancy recorder with an instantaneous read-out on command, of individual citizens' credit rating as well as the logging of debts against them.

Although the United States Post Office system appears to be as unlike the British Post Office as it is with respect to the Post Office system of most successful European giro countries, there appears to be no fundamental reason why the United States Post Office should not establish a National Giro on similar lines to that of our General Post Office. It would indeed be very appropriate if the U.S. Post Office were to follow Britain's example at a time when the affairs of the GPO are being organised by the American McKinsey consultancy group (Fig. 48).

The feature columnist of *The Financial Times*, Anthony Harris,

Is there anything in the 'Big Top'?

FIG. 48. This sketch from the pages of the journal of the National Federation of Sub-Postmasters was the first published cartoon using the National Giro as a theme for humour. It refers to feelings held in some quarters on the effects of appointing a group of American consultants to advise the Postmaster-General on organisation reform.

forecast in April 1967 that the pattern of banking emerging as the result of the impact made on modernisation of the banks by the National Giro "... in the next stage of this strategy, will serve as the most impressive possible shop-window for a U.S. sales drive."

Unless the American public is prepared to face the prospect of deteriorating banking standards, the menace of increased criminal use of banking services and the cost of mammoth computer systems to prop up the existing system, they would be well advised to press for the establishment of a coast-to-coast giro network. The alternatives present as many risks as cures and, to boot, a frighteningly costly investment in equipment and man-power which, in the path of a typhoon roaring across a dozen states—a not uncommon occurrence—could be brought to a crashing halt for half the country. Confusion is greater than in the United Kingdom because the United States of America has several hundred banking houses each with a small number of branches and the regulations governing the opening of a new branch have been so strict that it is almost easier to open a new banking house.

A comparison of banking costs to the customer, between American and Canadian banks, was made in the *National Bank Review*, v. 2, no. 3, pp. 399–401. An interesting observation made by one investigator was that the nationwide branching of Canadian banks lessens competition with the result that the customer pays more for services, although this assumption was not borne out by random sampling. Briefly, the comparative results obtained from an investigation of banks 25 miles apart, on either side of the frontier were:

1. An American bank at Niagara Falls, New York.
   (a) Cheque charge for *Special* or *Personal** account facilities: 15 cents per cheque.
   (b) Charge for *Regular* or *Current** account facilities: 75 cents for a deposit and 6 cents per entry for cheques drawn, with a minimum monthly balance holding at a rate of 20 cents per $100.
2. A Canadian bank at Niagara Falls, Ontario.
   (a) A cheque charge of 10 cents with no monthly mainte-nance or deposit charge.
   (b) A charge of 10 cents per entry, but with one free entry allowed for each $50 of balance held. Cheques drawn on savings accounts attract a charge of 15 cents each,

---

* Indicates the Canadian expression for each type of account. Figures are expressed in U.S. and Canadian dollars.

but there is an allowance of 1 free cheque per 3 months
for every $100 of balance.

If the American public could benefit from copying the British
interest in Post Office giro as a scientific solution to the banking
and money transfer problems of the latter third of the twentieth
century and beyond, the British banks might well benefit from
adopting some of the suggestions for extended services proposed
by Mr. Dale L. Reistad (see p.p. 221–3).

5.4.   Giro's Impact on Marketing Method and Office Management

Giro's greatest visible impact will be on business planning and
office administration.

In Sweden and West Germany, Holland and Switzerland, the
shape of commercial administration is already evolving for as far
ahead as the 1980's. But few British business equipment manufacturers, with the exception of such forward-looking companies as
Digico Ltd., (Letchworth), Creed, Bell and Howell, Kalamazoo,
the RUF Organisation, Thomas de la Rue, Kemp Application
Sales, Fanfold, and those supplying equipment for the National
Giro Centre, apparently have been thinking about the administrative schemes which will grow up to replace the humdrum and costly
manual methods which giro-based opportunities will replace.

According to a report produced by PA Management Consultants the cost of clerical work in Britain in 1964 was some £2000
million and there appeared to be no limit to the increase in these
costs, which are for work productive of little else than writing on
paper.

If British management reacts favourably to first a giro and then
to decimal currency the trend will be for a fairly rapid decline in
routine paperwork. Office staff will be replaced by fully or partially
automated machinery. Clerks and typists will be superseded by
administrators with technico-commercial qualifications, inspirational qualities, and self-reliance. Conversely, it will be increasingly
difficult for youngsters who have failed to make the best of their

opportunities whilst at school to "drift into" an office job. Even the days of the shorthand-typist were numbered when, about 1953–4, Professor Fry demonstrated in the Phonetics Department of London University an elementary voice-operated typewriter. Although the experiment fell short of what would be needed in place of a typist, the research model established what might develop.

Office hustle and bustle have for long been regarded as signs of work and effect, but this symbolic cult is likely to die out and be replaced by air-conditioned halls of computer-directed equipment integrated with slave-devices comprising a total complex of programmed administration charged with automatically maintaining and expanding a company's business.

Contrary to much popular belief, the advent of increased automation need not necessarily create less work for human beings; there will merely be a shift of emphasis, as when the vacuum cleaner and dishwasher replaced the housemaid. In Sweden the trend had been fostered by firms like Addo and Facit, which have made a point of designing office automation without dehumanisation. But even in Sweden, the trend towards mechanised business organisation is still in its infancy because, until the production of entirely reliable and inexpensive electronic microcircuit modules, the dream of what can be achieved to lift the load of boring and frustrating dead-end jobs off human shoulders has remained only a dream in electro–mechanical system designers' minds. The time is not far distant now when humdrum routines can be passed over entirely to machines, and people will be set free to work on inspirational tasks which will offer a greater financial and ethical reward than many jobs now done by pen-pushers and typewriter key tappers in millions of offices. Recent British advances in computer microcircuitry (Fig. 49)—such as the Mullard memory stores for computers—bring designers' dreams within the orbit of practicability.

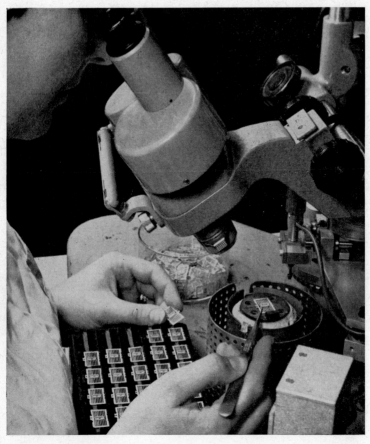

FIG. 49. Computerised banking and business system automation poses a challenge to British electronic engineers to invent smaller, speedier and more durable equipment. These silicon microcircuit modules under inspection at Mullard's Southampton works are a notable technological advance.

5.5.   The New Economy

This chapter was started when Britain was approaching the threshold of change from old to new, from a monetary and banking system shaped by historical events to a scientifically designed decimal currency and computer-actuated giro system. Between 1968 and 1972 the financial and economic institutions of the United Kingdom will undergo the greatest upheaval in history but, unlike the upheavals of war—which, formerly, has been the great force to set in motion the turbulence resulting in gargantuan national economic changes—this upheaval will be a planned one designed to lay the foundations of both a nationally efficient economy, and one that meets the needs of international commerce. It is likely to prove one of the most convincing examples of how modern technology can bring greater prosperity and improved living conditions to every member of the public.

At a time when electro–mechanical systems are proving so reliable that man is conquering the difficulties of flight beyond the Earth's atmosphere, and is reaching out to the planets and beyond, it would be inappropriate to speculate about all the effects which will result from the bold and timely decision to entrust Britain's future to these scientifically contrived monetary reforms, the foundations for a virulent new economy.

Bibliography

1. AUSTRIA

1.1. Official Publications: Österreichisches Postsparkassenamt, Georg Coch-Platz 2, Vienna 1.

    1.1.1. *Österreichisches Postsparkassenamt Geschäftsbericht*, published annually.

2. BRITAIN

2.1. Government Publications: Her Majesty's Stationery Office, Holborn, London, WC2.

    2.1.1. *The Working of the Monetary System*, Royal Commission Report, Cmnd. 827 (1959).

    2.1.2. *Parliamentary Debates (Hansard): House of Commons Official Reports* 21 July 1965, cols. 1589–1643; 20 January 1967, cols. 860–72, 880–91; 16 February 1967, cols. 770–1.

    2.1.3. *A Post Office Giro*, a white paper, Cmnd. 2751 (1965).

    2.1.4. *Decimal Currency in the United Kingdom*, Cmnd. 3164 (1966).

    2.1.5. *Bank Charges*, Cmnd. 3292 (1967).

2.2. Official Giro Publications: Directorate of Giro and Remittance Services, Empire House, St. Martin's-le-Grand, London, EC1.

    2.2.1. *The National Giro: The New Current Account Banking Service* (July 1966). Free on demand.

    2.2.2. *Giro: The Modern Banking Service* (October 1966). Free from the Post Office in selected areas.

2.3. Official Publications of the British Museum, Bloomsbury, London, WC1.

    2.3.1. *Melanesia—A Short Ethnography* by B. A. L. CRANSTON.

    2.3.2. *A Guide to the Primitive Coins of the Greeks*, by B. V. HEAD.

2.4. General Reference Books

    2.4.1. EINZIG, PAUL, *Primitive Money*, 2nd edn. Pergamon Press, Oxford (1966).

    2.4.2. THOMSON, F. P., *Giro Credit Transfer System*, Pergamon Press, Oxford (1964).

    2.4.3. COMMITTEE OF LONDON CLEARING BANKS, *Requirements for Automatic Cheque Processing*, London, EC3 (1962).

    2.4.4. TUC NON-MANUAL WORKERS' COMMITTEE, *In the Automated Office*, Trades Union Congress House, London WC1 (1964).

2.4.5. QUIGGIN, A. H., *A Survey of Primitive Money*, Methuen, London.
2.4.6. BRITISH COMPUTER SOCIETY, *Character Recognition: 1967 Report*, London, NW1.

2.5. Journal and Newspaper Articles

2.5.1. THORNTON, R. G., How would giro affect the banks? *The Times*, 31 December 1964, p. 14.
2.5.2. THORNTON, R. G., How would giro affect the banks in the U.K.? *J. Inst. Bankers* (*London*), Pt. I, pp. 15–18, February 1965.
2.5.3. JACOBS, ALAN, Advantages of a postal giro system, *The Times*, 19 January 1965, p. 16.
2.5.4. JACOBS, ALAN, Giro and venture at last, *Sub-Postmaster*, September 1965, pp. 214–15 and 222.
2.5.5. LOMBARD, Where the Post Office needs a new look, *The Financial Times*, 3 October 1964, p. 8, Oncoming giro—should banks and GPO join forces? *ibid.* 21 July 1965, p. 11. The banks and the giro —what kind of counter-action?, *ibid.*, 23 September 1965, p. 13, Off-loading the bother of paying wages in cash, *ibid.*, 10 July 1965, p. 8. Impact of giro on bank charges, *ibid.*, 24 July 1965, p. 8.
2.5.6. GORDON TETHER, C., Banks' unwise resistance to a matching Giro, *The Financial Times*, 25 November 1966, p. 13. PIB report—the bankers are not amused, *ibid.*, 1 June 1967, p. 15.
2.5.7. ROGALLY, JOE., Can the Post Office beat the banks? *The Financial Times*, 3 March 1967, p. 6.
2.5.8. A.S.M. Postgiro: will Britain adopt Sweden's system? *Anglo–Swedish Review*, April 1965.
2.5.9. LANE, N., Cheques, credit transfers and the giro, *Manager—J. Brit. Inst. Management*, April 1965, p. 1.
2.5.10. CASHDAN, D., Speeding the credit system, *The Birmingham Post*, 5 July 1965, p. 10.
2.5.11. COOPER, J., Watford man has shown the way, *West Herts. and Watford Observer*, 23 July 1965, p. 14.
2.5.12. ANON., Watford man puts giro on the map, *Watford and West Herts. Post*, 29 July 1965, p. 2.
2.5.13. MCDOWALL, K., Benn's Bank, *Daily Mail*, 22 July 1965, p. 9.
2.5.14. WOLFF, W. and SULLIVAN, D., Bank with giro—and pay those bills on a Post Office form, *Daily Mirror*, 22 July 1965, p. 9.
2.5.15. PAGE, R., Pay your bills at Post Office, *Sun*, 22 July 1965, p. 12.
2.5.16. ANON., Post office will run giro system, *Daily Telegraph*, 22 July 1965. 7 years of controversy over giro credit system, 22 July 1965, p. 27.
2.5.17. ANON., Enter the postal giro, *Daily Express*, 22 July 1965, p. 9.
2.5.18. THOMSON, F. P., Benn's bank, *J. Assoc. Sc. Workers*, May 1966, pp. 7–8. Giro banking plans, *ibid.*, November 1966, pp. 8–9.
2.5.19. STAINBANK, J. E., Giro banking plans, *J. Assoc. Sc. Workers*, January 1967, p. 17.
2.5.20. THOMSON, F. P., The erratic course of Britain's giro, *Belfast Telegraph*, 19 January 1967, p. 8.

2.5.21. THOMSON, F. P., Giro is the key to finance house efficiency, *Credit—Quarterly Rev. of Finance Houses Assoc.*, June 1965, pp. 45–51.
2.5.22. THOMSON, F. P., Benn's bank, *Plebs.*, November 1965, pp. 23–5. Giro bank, October 1966, pp. 24–5. More on giro, *ibid.*, December 1966, pp. 28–9.
2.5.23. THOMSON, F. P., Giro bank plans, *J. Royal Soc. Arts*, November 1966, pp. 1033–4.
2.5.24. THOMSON, F. P., Broken promises?, *Socialist Commentary*, December 1966, pp. 22–3.
2.5.25. MORRIS, CHARLES, M.P., The British giro, *Socialist Commentary*, March 1967, pp. 17–18.
2.5.26. WISE, MERVYN, Post Office giro, *Socialist Commentary*, June 1967, p. 31.
2.5.27. THOMSON, F. P., Giro as a crime deterrent, *The Police Journal*, June 1967, pp. 276–80.
2.5.28. THOMSON, F. P., Giro: Britain's quietest reform, *Sibford School O.S. Magazine*, Sibford Ferris, near Banbury, Oxon. 1966 issue, pp. 29–32.
2.5.29. THOMSON, F. P., Giro as key to European computer utilisation progress, *J. Radar Electronics Assoc. (London)*, Spring issue, 1967, pp. 17–27.
2.5.30. THOMSON, F. P., The National Giro, *J. International Accountants Assoc. (London)*, December 1966, p. 122.
2.5.31. THOMSON, F. P., The National Giro, *J. Economics Assoc.*, Spring issue, 1967, pp. 11–17.
2.5.32. HARRIS, B., Are you happy with the way your bank treats you? *Sunday Express*, 7 February 1965, p. 26.
2.5.33. ANON., *The GPO Gets With It*, election pamphlet, Labour Party, London, SW1, March 1966.
2.5.34. EDITORIAL, Commentary, *Electronic Components (London)*, August 1967, p. 857; September 1967, p. 953.

3. BELGIUM

3.1. Official Publications: Ministère des Postes, Télégraphes et Téléphones, Office des Chèques Postaux, Rue de Louvain 86, Brussels 1.
3.1.1. *Rapport Annuel.*

4. DENMARK

4.1. Official Publications: General Directorate of Posts and Telegraphs, Ministry of Public Works, Tietgensgade 37, Copenhagen.
4.1.1. *Postgirobogen*, published annually.

5. FINLAND

5.1. Official Publications: Postisäästöpankki, Unionkatu 20, Helsinki.
5.1.1. *Postisiirtotillit*, published annually.

234 BIBLIOGRAPHY

6. FRANCE

6.1. Official Publications: Direction de la Caisse Nationale d'Épargne, Des Chèques Postaux et des Articles d'Argent, 20 Avenue Ségur, Paris 7e.
    6.1.1. *Les Chèques Postaux.*

7. WEST GERMANY

7.1. Official Publications: Der Bundesminister für das Post- und Fernmelde-wesen, Koblenzer Strasse 81 (53) Bonn.
    7.1.1. *Annual Report of the Deutsche Bundespost*, published in English.

8. HOLLAND

8.1. Official Publications: The Netherlands Postal and Telecommunications Service, 11/12 Kortenaerkade, The Hague.
    8.1.1. *A Short Survey: Postal Cheque and Giro Service in Holland* (in English).

9. ITALY

9.1. Official Publications: Ministero delle Poste e delle Telecommunicazioni, Direzione Centrale dei Conti Correnti Postali, Rome.
    9.1.1. *Guida Practica ad Uso del Correntista Postale*, published annually.

10. GRAND DUCHY OF LUXEMBOURG

10.1. Official Publications: Administration des Postes, Télégraphes et Télé-phones, Luxembourg.
    10.1.1. *Rapport de Gestion* published annually.

11. NEW ZEALAND

11.1. Journal Articles.
    11.1.1. THOMSON, F. P., Giro banking: a British reform that could benefit New Zealand, *Management—J. N.Z. Inst. Management*, March 1967, pp. 19–25.

12. NORWAY

12.1. Official Publications: Postgirokontoret, Tollbugt. 17, Oslo.
    12.1.1. *Annual Statistics of the Postgiro Service.*

13. SWEDEN

13.1. Official Publications: Postgirokontoret, Klarabergsgatan 60, Stockholm.
13.1.1. *Postbanken i Ny Miljö Efter 80 år i Sparandets Tjänst.*
13.1.2. *Postbankens Verksamhets Berättelse*, published annually.
13.1.3. *Postbanken Report*, published annually in English.

14. SWITZERLAND

14.1. Official Publications: Post, Telephone, and Telegraph Administration, Bollwerk 25, Berne.
14.1.1. *Étude Sur L'Automatisation du Service des Chèques Postaux.*
14.1.2. *Annual Statistics.*

15. UNITED STATES OF AMERICA

15.1. Official Publications: Federal Reserve Bank of Richmond, Virginia 23213.
15.1.1. *Readings on Money.*
15.2. Reference Books.
15.2.1. AMERICAN BANKERS' ASSOCIATION, *Proceedings, National Automation Conference* 1965., A.B. Assoc. N.Y.
15.2.2. BOARD OF GOVERNORS, *The Federal Reserve System: Purposes and Functions 1913–63*, Federal Reserve System, Washington, D.C.
15.2.3. SUBCOMMITTEE ON DOMESTIC FINANCE, COMMITTEE ON BANKING AND CURRENCY, HOUSE OF REPRESENTATIVES, 88th CONGRESS, U.S.A., *Comparative Regulations of Financial Institutions.*
15.2.4. FEDERAL RESERVE BANK OF NEW YORK, *Functional Cost Analysis 1963–4 Comparative Study: 34 Banks With Deposits Over 50 Million.*
15.2.5. FEDERAL RESERVE BANK OF NEW YORK, *Performance Characteristics of High Earning Banks: Functional Cost Analysis—1964.*

16. UNIVERSAL POSTAL UNION

16.1. Official Publications: UPU, Berne, Switzerland.
16.1.1. *Statistique des Services Postaux*, published annually.

17. EUROPEAN COMPUTER MANUFACTURERS ASSOCIATION

17.1. Official Publications: ECMA, Rue d'Italie 11, 1204 Geneva, Switzerland.
17.1.1. *ECMA Standard for the CMC7 Printed Image Specification.*
17.1.2. *Comments and Notes on the Standard ECMA–3 For the Printed Image of the CMC7 Font.*

18. INDIA

18.1. Journal Articles.
18.1.1 THOMSON, F. P., Giro banking: a British reform that could benefit Indian economy, *Artha-Vikas—the Indian Journal of Economic Development* (Sardar Patel University), July 1967, pp. 42–58.

Index

237